P9-DUY-702

DAYBOOK

OF CRITICAL READING AND WRITING

daybook, n. a book in which the events of the day are recorded; specif. a journal or diary

THE AUTHORS:
* Fran Claggett
* Louann Reid
* Ruth Vinz

Great Source Education Group
A division of Houghton Mifflin Company
Wilmington, Massachusetts

THE AUTHORS

✳ **Fran Claggett**, an educational consultant, writer, and teacher at Sonoma State University, taught high school and college English for more than thirty years. Her books include *Drawing Your Own Conclusions: Graphic Strategies for Reading, Writing, and Thinking* (1992) with Joan Brown, *A Measure of Success* (1996), and *Teaching Writing: Art, Craft, and Genre* (2005) with Joan Brown, Nancy Patterson, and Louann Reid.

✳ **Louann Reid** taught junior and senior high school English for nineteen years and currently teaches courses for future English teachers at Colorado State University. She has edited *English Journal* and is the author or editor of several books and articles, including *Learning the Landscape and Recasting the Text* (1996) with Fran Claggett and Ruth Vinz. She is a frequent consultant and workshop presenter nationally and internationally.

✳ **Ruth Vinz**, currently a professor of English education and Morse Chair in Teacher Education at Teachers College, Columbia University, taught in secondary schools for twenty-three years. She is author of numerous books and articles that focus on teaching and learning in the English classroom. Dr. Vinz is a frequent presenter at conferences as well as a consultant and co-teacher in schools throughout the country.

REVIEWERS

Maureen Akin
Houston ISD
Houston, TX

Marla Kay Dandrea
Gahanna-Jefferson
Public Schools
Gahanna, OH

Mary Fran Ennis
Lake Stevens School
District
Lake Stevens, WA

Patricia A. Fair
Cherry Creek Public
Schools
Greenwood Village, CO

Jenny R. May
Mason City Schools
Mason, OH

Connie McGee
Miami-Dade County
Public Schools
Miami, FL

Marie T. Raduazzo
Arlington Public Schools
Arlington, MA

Elizabeth A. Rehberger
Huntington Beach High
School
Huntington Beach, CA

EDITORIAL: Barbara Levadi and Sue Paro
DESIGN AND PRODUCTION: AARTPACK, Inc.

Copyright © 2007 by Great Source Education Group, a division of Houghton Mifflin Company. All rights reserved.

No part of this work may be reproduced or transmitted in any form or by any means, electronic or mechanical, including photocopying and recording, or by any information storage or retrieval system without the prior written permission of the copyright owner unless such copying is expressly permitted by federal copyright law. With the exception of non-profit transcription in Braille, Great Source Education Group is not authorized to grant permission for further uses of copyrighted selections reprinted in this text without the permission of their owners. Permission must be obtained from the individual copyright owners as identified herein. Address requests for permission to make copies of Great Source material only to Great Source Education Group, 181 Ballardvale Street, Wilmington, MA 01887.

Great Source ® is a registered trademark of Houghton Mifflin Company.

Printed in the United States of America

International Standard Book Number 13: 978-0-669-53485-6

International Standard Book Number 10: 0-669-53485-4

1 2 3 4 5 6 7 8 9 10 - VH - 11 10 09 08 07 06

Contents

© GREAT SOURCE. COPYING IS PROHIBITED.

Focus/Skill		Selection/Author	

© GREAT SOURCE. COPYING IS PROHIBITED.

Focus/Skill		Selection/Author	

© GREAT SOURCE. COPYING IS PROHIBITED.

Focus/Skill		Selection/Author	

© GREAT SOURCE. COPYING IS PROHIBITED.

© GREAT SOURCE. COPYING IS PROHIBITED.

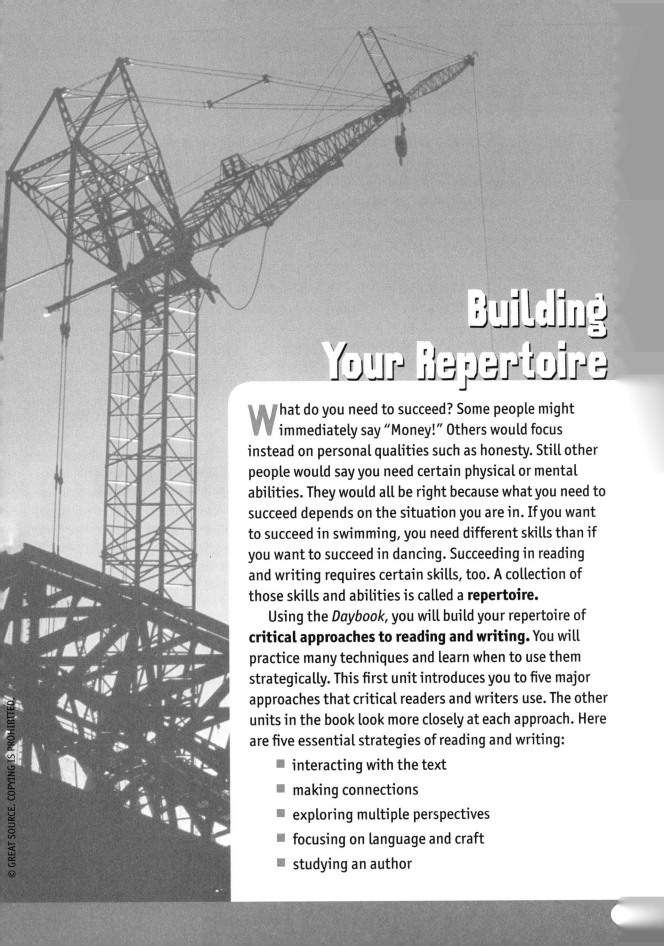

Building Your Repertoire

What do you need to succeed? Some people might immediately say "Money!" Others would focus instead on personal qualities such as honesty. Still other people would say you need certain physical or mental abilities. They would all be right because what you need to succeed depends on the situation you are in. If you want to succeed in swimming, you need different skills than if you want to succeed in dancing. Succeeding in reading and writing requires certain skills, too. A collection of those skills and abilities is called a **repertoire.**

Using the *Daybook,* you will build your repertoire of **critical approaches to reading and writing.** You will practice many techniques and learn when to use them strategically. This first unit introduces you to five major approaches that critical readers and writers use. The other units in the book look more closely at each approach. Here are five essential strategies of reading and writing:

- interacting with the text
- making connections
- exploring multiple perspectives
- focusing on language and craft
- studying an author

© GREAT SOURCE. COPYING IS PROHIBITED.

When you **interact with a text,** you have a conversation with it. The text is one side of the conversation. For your part of the conversation, take your pen and mark up the page as you respond to the text. Make up a code to show how your mind works. Underline parts you like. Use ??? for parts that confuse you, or xxx for parts that upset you, or !!! for parts that surprise you. Add comments such as "Why?" "I don't think so," "I wonder. . . ." Your writing captures your thinking right on the page.

In the *Daybook*, use the **Response Notes** column to help you talk, or converse, with the text as you read. Here's how one reader used the space.

from **A Summer Life** by Gary Soto

Response Notes

Sounds like a song —I like it.

What's this about?
Understatement!

In high school, girls were blossoms shaken from a tree and blooming with life. We didn't know how to talk to them, so we rehearsed by the school fountain. "Do you go to this school?" Scott asked, and I punched him in the arm. "Of course they do. Why else would they be here?"

I tried, "I walked by your house and saw that you have a palm tree. I have a palm tree. What a coincidence."

Scott tried: "It's cold for December."

I tried: "A June bug can live on a screen door for days."

Scott tried: "It rains a lot in April, but the funny thing is the rain is either very cold or very warm but never in between." *???*

I tried: "My friend Tony said he would take the bullet for the president."

Scott tried: "Chicken is my favorite food."

We needed help. ❖

© GREAT SOURCE. COPYING IS PROHIBITED.

Gary Soto often writes about boy-girl relationships. As you read the first part of a short story by him, mark it up to show questions, ideas, and any other responses you have.

"Seventh Grade" by Gary Soto

On the first day of school, Victor stood in line half an hour before he came to a wobbly card table. He was handed a packet of papers and a computer card on which he listed his one elective, French. He already spoke Spanish and English, but he thought someday he might travel to France, where it was cool; not like Fresno, where summer days reached 110 degrees in the shade. There were rivers in France, and huge churches, and fair-skinned people every- where, the way there were brown people all around Victor.

Besides, Teresa, a girl he had liked since they were in catechism classes at Saint Theresa's, was taking French, too. With any luck they would be in the same class. Teresa is going to be my girl this year, he promised himself as he left the gym full of students in their new fall clothes. She was cute. And good at math, too, Victor thought as he walked down the hall to his homeroom. He ran into his friend, Michael Torres, by the water fountain that never turned off.

They shook hands, *raza*-style, and jerked their heads at one another in a *saludo de vato.* "How come you're making a face?" asked Victor.

"I ain't making a face, *ese.* This *is* my face." Michael said his face had changed during the summer. He had read a *GQ* magazine that his older brother borrowed from the Book Mobile and noticed that the male models all had the same look on their faces. They would stand, one arm around a beautiful woman, and *scowl.* They would sit at a pool, their rippled stomachs dark with shadow, and *scowl.* They would sit at dinner tables, cool drinks in their hands, and *scowl.*

"I think it works," Michael said. He scowled and let his upper lip quiver. His teeth showed along with the ferocity of his soul. "Belinda Reyes walked by a while ago and looked at me," he said.

Victor didn't say anything, though he thought his friend looked pretty strange. They talked about recent movies, baseball, their parents, and the horrors of picking grapes in order to buy their fall clothes. Picking grapes was like living in Siberia, except hot and more boring. "simily"

"What classes are you taking?" Michael said, scowling.

"French. How 'bout you?"

"Spanish. I ain't so good at it, even if I'm Mexican."

"I'm not either, but I'm better at it than math, that's for sure."

A tinny, three-beat bell propelled students to their homerooms. The two friends socked each other in the arm and went their ways, Victor thinking, man, that's weird. Michael thinks making a face makes him handsome.

© GREAT SOURCE. COPYING IS PROHIBITED.

Victors in the seventh grade and hes already dreaming about traveling to France.

"Raza-style" that caught my eye because it relates to my culture. im used to that kind of slang.

what is scowling?? i dont know what that means.

The students

On the way to his homeroom, Victor tried a scowl. He felt foolish, until out of the corner of his eye he saw a girl looking at him. Umm, he thought, maybe it does work. He scowled with greater conviction.

In homeroom, roll was taken, emergency cards were passed out, and they were given a bulletin to take home to their parents. The principal, Mr. Belton, spoke over the crackling loudspeaker, welcoming the students to a new year, new experiences, and new friendships. The students squirmed in their chairs and ignored him. They were anxious to go to first period. Victor sat calmly, thinking of Teresa, who sat two rows away, reading a paperback novel. This would be his lucky year. She was in his homeroom, and would probably be in his English and math classes. And, of course, French. ✛

✶ Write your initial impressions of this story. What do you think of it?

_____

_____

_____

✶ Compare your impressions and your **Response Notes** with a partner or small group. What questions do you have about the story or author? After your discussion, do a quick-write to explore one of your questions about what you've read so far or about Gary Soto's writing.

_____

_____

_____

_____

_____

_____

_____

_____

Interact with the text by marking it up with ideas, questions, and comments as you read.

_____

_____

© GREAT SOURCE. COPYING IS PROHIBITED.

ary Soto's first writings were poems. He recalls, "I once worked on a single fourteen-line poem for a week, changing verbs, reworking line breaks, cutting out unnecessary words." He then explains, "Poetry is a concentrated form of writing; so much meaning is packed into such a little space. Therefore, each word in a poem is very important and is chosen very carefully to convey just the right meaning." Choosing the right word is part of Gary Soto's repertoire as a writer. What he says can apply to all writing, not just poetry. Authors craft their work carefully, **choosing words** to create strong images, express ideas, and spark feelings.

Gary Soto sees his readers as his teammates: "You have to concentrate when you read a poem, just as you must concentrate when you're in the batter's box and your team needs you to bring in a player from second base." Take Soto's advice as you read "Oranges." Read it at least twice. Interact with the text as you read—underline words or phrases that strike you. Put a question mark next to anything that you wonder about. Another way to interact with the text is to visualize what you're reading, so use the **Response Notes** for drawings or rough sketches of what you see in your mind as you read.

Oranges by Gary Soto

The first time I walked
With a girl, I was twelve,
Cold, and weighted down
With two oranges in my jacket.
December. Frost cracking
Beneath my steps, my breath
Before me, then gone,
As I walked toward
Her house, the one whose
Porch light burned yellow
Night and day, in any weather.
A dog barked at me, until
She came out pulling
At her gloves, face bright
With rouge. I smiled,
Touched her shoulder, and led ▶▶▶

Response Notes

© GREAT SOURCE. COPYING IS PROHIBITED.

Her down the street, across
A used car lot and a line
Of newly planted trees,
Until we were breathing
Before a drugstore. We
Entered, the tiny bell
Bringing a saleslady
Down a narrow aisle of goods.
I turned to the candies
Tiered like bleachers,
And asked what she wanted —
Light in her eyes, a smile
Starting at the corners
Of her mouth. I fingered
A nickel in my pocket,
And when she lifted a chocolate
That cost a dime,
I didn't say anything.
I took the nickel from
My pocket, then an orange,
And set them quietly on
The counter. When I looked up,
The lady's eyes met mine,
And held them, knowing
Very well what it was all
About.
             Outside,
A few cars hissing past,
Fog hanging like old
Coats between the trees.
I took my girl's hand
In mine for two blocks,
Then released it to let
Her unwrap the chocolate.
I peeled my orange
That was so bright against
The gray of December
That, from some distance,
Someone might have thought
I was making a fire in my hands. ❖

© GREAT SOURCE. COPYING IS PROHIBITED.

✳ What line or small section of the poem was most vivid for you? Put a box around it and then, in the space below, explain why you selected it.

_____

_____

_____

_____

✳ "Oranges" and "Seventh Grade" show boys making friends with girls. Skim both selections again. Fill in the chart to compare some of the elements of craft that you find in each. (Not all of the elements will be present in both pieces.)

Elements of craft	"Oranges"	"Seventh Grade"
strong images		
vivid descriptions of feelings		
humorous phrases or expressions		
realistic characterization		

Focusing on the words and sentences helps you understand an author's ideas and individual style.

FOCUSING ON LANGUAGE AND CRAFT 21

© GREAT SOURCE. COPYING IS PROHIBITED.

Readers are often curious about how much of an author's life goes into the stories and poems he or she writes. Some authors use more autobiographical material than others, but you cannot just assume that a poem or story written in the first person (using *I, me, we,* or *us*) is autobiographical. However, a small kernel of real-life experience may provide a starting point for a work of fiction.

Read the selection below, which describes Gary Soto's memories of picking grapes to earn money for school clothes. This piece *is* autobiographical, and you may find connections between it and the two selections you have already read—"Oranges" and "Seventh Grade." Read actively by writing your own comments and connections in the **Response Notes**.

Response Notes

Soto creates images here, as he did in "Oranges."

from **Living Up the Street** by Gary Soto

I cut another bunch, then another, fighting the snap and whip of vines. After ten minutes of groping for grapes, my first pan brimmed with bunches. I poured them on the paper tray, which was bordered by a wooden frame that kept the grapes from rolling off, and they spilled like jewels from a pirate's chest. The tray was only half filled, so I hurried to jump under the vines and begin groping, cutting, and tugging at the grapes again. I emptied the pan, raked the grapes with my hands to make them look like they filled the tray, and jumped back under the vine on my knees. I tried to cut faster because Mother, in the next row, was slowly moving ahead. I peeked into her row and saw five trays gleaming in the early morning. I cut, pulled hard, and stopped to gather the grapes that missed the pan; already bored, I spat on a few to wash them before tossing them like popcorn into my mouth.

So it went. Two pans equaled one tray—or six cents. By lunchtime I had a trail of thirty-seven trays behind me while Mother had sixty or more. We met about halfway from our last trays, and I sat down with a grunt, knees wet from kneeling on dropped grapes. I washed my hands with the water from the jug, drying them on the inside of my shirt sleeve before I opened the paper bag for the first sandwich, which I gave to Mother. I dipped my hand in again to unwrap a sandwich without looking at it. I took a first bite and chewed it slowly for the tang of mustard. Eating in silence I looked straight ahead at the vines, and only when we were finished with cookies did we talk.

"Are you tired?" she asked.

© GREAT SOURCE. COPYING IS PROHIBITED.

"No, but I got a sliver from the frame," I told her. I showed her the web of skin between my thumb and index finger. She wrinkled her forehead but said it was nothing.

"How many trays did you do?"

I looked straight ahead, not answering at first. I recounted in my mind the whole morning of bend, cut, pour again and again, before answering a feeble "thirty-seven." No elaboration, no detail. Without looking at me she told me how she had done field work in Texas and Michigan as a child. But I had a difficult time listening to her stories. I played with my grape knife, stabbing it into the ground, but stopped when Mother reminded me that I had better not lose it. I left the knife sticking up like a small, leafless plant. She then talked about school, the junior high I would be going to that fall, and then about Rick and Debra [Soto's brother and sister], how sorry they would be that they hadn't come out to pick grapes because they'd have no new clothes for the school year. She stopped talking when she peeked at her watch, a bandless one she kept in her pocket. She got up with an *"Ay, Dios,"* and told me that we'd work until three, leaving me cutting figures in the sand with my knife and dreading the return to work.

Finally I rose and walked slowly back to where I had left off, again kneeling under the vine and fixing the pan under bunches of grapes. By that time, 11:30, the sun was over my shoulder and made me squint and think of the pool at the Y.M.C.A. where I was a summer member. I saw myself diving face first into the water and loving it. I saw myself gleaming like something new, at the edge of the pool. I had to daydream and keep my mind busy because boredom was a terror almost as awful as the work itself. My mind went dumb with stupid things, and I had to keep it moving with dreams of baseball and would-be girlfriends. I even sang, however softly, to keep my mind moving, my hands moving.

I worked less hurriedly and with less vision. I no longer saw that copper pot sitting squat on our stove or Mother waiting for it to whistle. The wardrobe that I imagined, crisp and bright in the closet, numbered only one pair of jeans and two shirts because, in half a day, six cents times thirty-seven trays was two dollars and twenty-two cents. It became clear to me. If I worked eight hours, I might make four dollars. ❖

❊ Discuss with a partner any connections you find between Gary Soto's life and his writing. Label the parts of the excerpt from *Living Up the Street* that connect with "Oranges" and "Seventh Grade."

© GREAT SOURCE. COPYING IS PROHIBITED.

The more you know about how an author thinks, the more insight you will have into his or her writing. Read these quotes from Gary Soto. How have you seen his perspective reflected in his writing?

from an interview in *Contemporary Authors* by Jean W. Ross
"I like the youth in my poetry, sort of a craziness. For me that's really important. I don't want to take a dreary look at the world and then start writing."

from *A Fire in My Hands* by Gary Soto
"I tried to remain faithful to the common things of my childhood—dogs, alleys, my baseball mitt, curbs, and the fruit of the valley, especially the orange. I wanted to give these things life, to write so well that my poems would express their simple beauty."

from *California Childhood* by Gary Soto
"Childhood is not only place, but a response toward place. I'm speaking of fear and boredom, the sense of resignation in a poor family, the utter joy of jumping into cold river water, the loneliness of no girlfriend or boyfriend, envy of the rich in 'fresh' clothes, adolescent rebellion—human feelings that move beyond the borders of California to embrace all children."

Gary Soto mentions four elements that make up his perspective:

- a youthful quality, "sort of a craziness"
- an upbeat approach, the opposite of "a dreary look at the world"
- attention to the "simple beauty" of commonplace things and events
- a focus on young people's emotions

✳ Imagine that you have been asked to introduce Gary Soto to a group of students who will read some of his work. Choose one aspect of Soto's writing that is most interesting to you and write a short introduction.

_____

_____

_____

_____

_____

_____

_____

Studying an author's life and perspective can give you insights into his or her writing.

© GREAT SOURCE. COPYING IS PROHIBITED.

Interacting with the Text

Good readers develop skills and strategies to help them understand what they read. A skill is something you can do, like shooting a basket or solving a math problem. A strategy is the plan you make to accomplish a goal. In basketball, deciding to shoot a lay-up instead of making a jump shot is a strategy you choose because you know you are more likely to make that shot. In math, you might use a guess-and-check strategy instead of pencil and paper to solve your math problem because you know that you'll solve the problem more easily.

Strategic reading, or making decisions about how to approach a text, helps you interact with the text. In this unit, you will practice several strategies you can use when you read:

- making predictions
- questioning the text
- summarizing
- visualizing
- reflecting

The selections are about people who face difficult situations and act in remarkable ways. Although you may never have been in their situations, making personal connections with the texts and the characters will help you better understand their choices and actions.

Strategic readers **make predictions** about many things, such as what might happen next, what kind of person a character will turn out to be, or how the story will end. When you make a prediction, you use clues from what you have already read to make an educated guess about what you will read. Before you read, you might choose to read the title of a story and then predict what the story will be about. While you are reading, you might take what you know about the events of a story to predict what will happen next. As you continue to read, you test your predictions against what happens, you change them as necessary, and then you make new predictions. Predictions keep you thinking ahead. They also keep you connected to what you have read before.

As you read the selection below about a girl in Afghanistan, make predictions in the **Response Notes** and test them as you read. When you find something that either supports your prediction or makes you think another way, make a note of that.

If you come across unfamiliar words, circle them and read on to see if the context of the rest of the story helps you make sense of them.

from **The Breadwinner** by Deborah Ellis

Head covering?

"I can read that letter as well as Father can," Parvana whispered into the folds of her chador. "Well, almost."

She didn't dare say those words out loud. The man sitting beside her father would not want to hear her voice. Nor would anyone else in the Kabul market. Parvana was there only to help her father walk to the market and back home again after work. She sat well back on the blanket, her head and most of her face covered by her chador.

She wasn't really supposed to be outside at all. The Taliban had ordered all the girls and women in Afghanistan to stay inside their homes. They even forbade girls to go to school. Parvana had had to leave her sixth grade class, and her sister Nooria was not allowed to go to her high school. Their mother had been kicked out of her job as a writer for a Kabul radio station. For more than a year now, they had all been stuck inside one room, along with five-year-old Maryam and two-year-old Ali.

Parvana did get out for a few hours most days to help her father walk. She was always glad to go outside, even though it meant sitting for hours on a blanket spread over the hard ground of the marketplace. At least it was something to do. She had even got used to holding her tongue and hiding her face.

© GREAT SOURCE. COPYING IS PROHIBITED.

She was small for her eleven years. As a small girl, she could usually get away with being outside without being questioned.

"I need this girl to help me walk," her father would tell any Talib who asked, pointing to his leg. He had lost the lower part of his leg when the high school he was teaching in was bombed. His insides had been hurt somehow, too. He was often tired.

"I have no son at home, except for an infant," he would explain. Parvana would slump down further on the blanket and try to make herself look smaller. She was afraid to look up at the soldiers. She had seen what they did, especially to women, the way they would whip and beat someone they thought should be punished.

Sitting in the marketplace day after day, she had seen a lot. When the Taliban were around, what she wanted most of all was to be invisible.

Now the customer asked her father to read his letter again. "Read it slowly, so that I can remember it for my family."

Parvana would have liked to get a letter. Mail delivery had recently started again in Afghanistan, after years of being disrupted by war. Many of her friends had fled the country with their families. She thought they were in Pakistan, but she wasn't sure, so she couldn't write to them. Her own family had moved so often because of the bombing that her friends no longer knew where she was. "Afghans cover the earth like stars cover the sky," her father often said.

Her father finished reading the man's letter a second time. The customer thanked him and paid. "I will look for you when it is time to write a reply."

Most people in Afghanistan could not read or write. Parvana was one of the lucky ones. Both of her parents had been to university, and they believed in education for everyone, even girls. ❖

✳ Now that you have read the first few pages of the book, who do you think is "the breadwinner" of the family? Briefly tell why you think so.

_____

_____

_____

_____

_____

_____

© GREAT SOURCE. COPYING IS PROHIBITED.

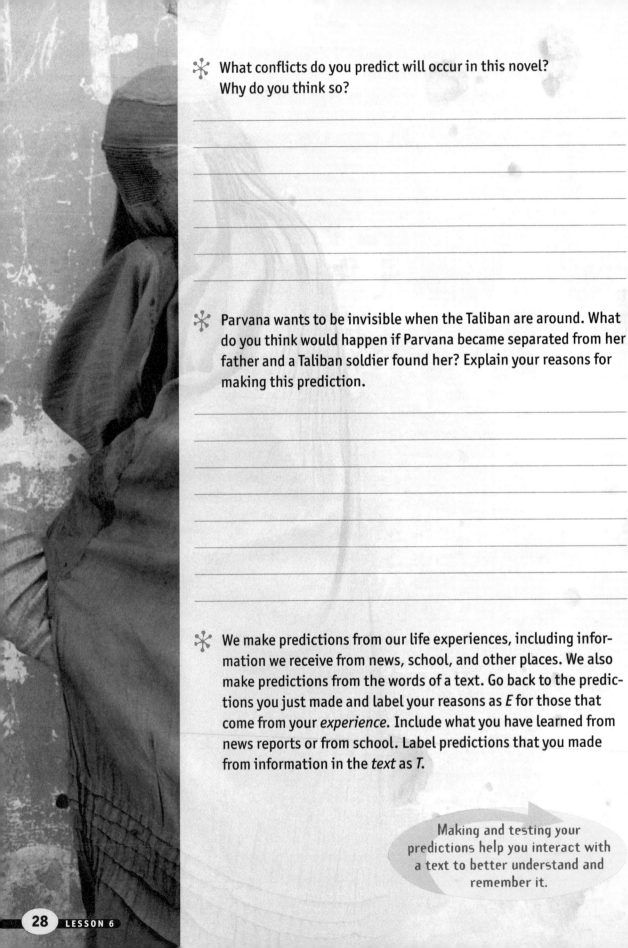

✳ What conflicts do you predict will occur in this novel?
Why do you think so?

_____

_____

_____

_____

_____

_____

✳ Parvana wants to be invisible when the Taliban are around. What
do you think would happen if Parvana became separated from her
father and a Taliban soldier found her? Explain your reasons for
making this prediction.

_____

_____

_____

_____

_____

_____

_____

_____

✳ We make predictions from our life experiences, including information we receive from news, school, and other places. We also
make predictions from the words of a text. Go back to the predictions you just made and label your reasons as _E_ for those that
come from your _experience_. Include what you have learned from
news reports or from school. Label predictions that you made
from information in the _text_ as _T_.

Making and testing your
predictions help you interact with
a text to better understand and
remember it.

© GREAT SOURCE. COPYING IS PROHIBITED.

Another way of reading strategically is to **ask questions** before, during, and after you read. Questions serve different purposes. One purpose is to ask about a fact or definition. For example, in the first lesson, you might have asked "What is a *chador*?" and found out that it is a cloth that women wear to cover their head and shoulders. Asking questions helps to build your understanding as you read. Questions that build understanding usually cannot be answered *yes* or *no*. You ask and answer them based on the information you encounter before, during, and after reading the text.

As you read the next part of the story, ask questions about the characters, the action, the author's reasons for writing as she did, and anything else that you wonder about. Write your questions in the **Response Notes**. The action in this part of the novel takes place in the evening after Parvana and her father return home from the marketplace. The family has had dinner and everyone is laughing at a funny face that Parvana made when she was told to do the dishes.

from **The Breadwinner** by Deborah Ellis

The whole family was laughing when four Taliban soldiers burst through the door.

Ali was the first to react. The slam of the door against the wall shocked him, and he screamed.

Mother leapt to her feet, and in an instant Ali and Maryam were in a corner of the room, shrieking behind her legs.

Nooria covered herself completely with her chador and scrunched herself into a small ball. Young women were sometimes stolen by soldiers. They were snatched from their homes, and their families never saw them again.

Parvana couldn't move. She sat as if frozen at the edge of the supper cloth. The soldiers were giants, their piled-high turbans making them look even taller.

Two of the soldiers grabbed her father. The other two began searching the apartment, kicking the remains of dinner all over the mat.

"Leave him alone!" Mother screamed. "He has done nothing wrong!"

"Why did you go to England for your education?" the soldiers yelled at Father. "Afghanistan doesn't need your foreign ideas!" They yanked him toward the door.

"Afghanistan needs more illiterate thugs like you," Father said. One of the soldiers hit him in the face. Blood from his nose dripped onto his white shalwar kameez.

Response Notes

How did the author get the information to write about this experience?

© GREAT SOURCE. COPYING IS PROHIBITED.

Mother sprang at the soldiers, pounding them with her fists. She grabbed Father's arm and tried to pull him out of their grasp.

One of the soldiers raised his rifle and whacked her on the head. She collapsed on the floor. The soldier hit her a few more times. Maryam and Ali screamed with every blow to their mother's back.

Seeing her mother on the ground finally propelled Parvana into action. When the soldiers dragged her father outside, she flung her arms around his waist. As the soldiers pried her loose, she heard her father say, "Take care of the others, my Malali." Then he was gone.

Parvana watched helplessly as two soldiers dragged him down the steps, his beautiful shalwar kameez ripping on the rough cement. Then they turned a corner, and she could see them no more.

Inside the room, the other two soldiers were ripping open the toshaks with knives and tossing things out of the cupboard.

Father's books! At the bottom of the cupboard was a secret compartment her father had built to hide the few books that had not been destroyed in one of the bombings. Some were English books about history and literature. They were kept hidden because the Taliban burned books they didn't like.

They couldn't be allowed to find Father's books! The soldiers had started at the top of the cupboard and were working their way down. Clothes, blankets, pots—everything landed on the floor.

Closer and closer they came to the bottom shelf, the one with the false wall. Parvana watched in horror as the soldiers bent down to yank the things out of the bottom shelf.

"Get out of my house!" she yelled. She threw herself at the soldiers with such force that they both fell to the ground. She swung at them with her fists until she was knocked aside. She heard rather than felt the thwack of their sticks on her back. She kept her head hidden in her arms until the beating stopped and the soldiers went away.

GREAT SOURCE. COPYING IS PROHIBITED

Mother got off the floor and had her hands full with Ali. Nooria was still curled up in a terrified ball. It was Maryam who came over to help Parvana.

At the first touch of her sister's hands, Parvana flinched, thinking it was the soldiers. Maryam kept stroking her hair until Parvana realized who it was. She sat up, aching all over. She and Maryam clung to each other, trembling.

She had no idea how long the family stayed like that. They remained in their spots long after Ali stopped screaming and collapsed into sleep. ❖

✳ Share your questions with a partner and try to answer each other's questions. List two of the questions you would like to discuss in class.

_____

_____

_____

_____

_____

_____

_____

_____

✳ Briefly explain how asking questions before, during, and after you read helped you understand the selection.

_____

_____

_____

_____

_____

_____

_____

_____

_____

> Strategic readers ask questions before, during, and after reading to build their understanding of what they read.

© GREAT SOURCE. COPYING IS PROHIBITED.

eaders show that they understand the main ideas and supporting details when they **summarize** what they read. Finding the main ideas and restating them in your own words is a strategy for you to use when you want to remember key points or ideas.

Sojourner Truth, an African American woman, spoke at a women's rights convention in 1851. Read her speech once to get an idea about the general subject.

✳ When you look at the title and know where and when she gave this speech, what do you predict will be her main point?

_____

_____

"Ain't I a Woman?" by Sojourner Truth

Response Notes

Well, children, where there is so much racket there must be something out of kilter. I think that 'twixt the Negroes of the South and the women at the North, all talking about rights, the white men will be in a fix pretty soon. But what's all this here talking about? That man over there says that women need to be helped into carriages, and lifted over ditches, and to have the best place everywhere. Nobody ever helps me into carriages, or over mud-puddles, or gives me any best place! And ain't I a woman? Look at me! Look at my arm! I have plowed and planted, and gathered into barns, and no man could head me! And ain't I a woman? I could work as much and eat as much as a man—when I could get it—and bear the lash as well! And ain't I a woman? I have borne thirteen children, and seen them most all sold off to slavery, and when I cried out with my mother's grief, none but Jesus heard! And ain't I a woman?

Then they talk about this thing in the head; what's this they call it? ["Intellect," someone in the audience whispers.] That's it, honey. What's that got to do with women's rights or Negro's rights? If my cup won't hold but a pint, and yours holds a quart, wouldn't you be mean not to let me have my little halfmeasure full? Then that little man in black there, he says women can't have as much rights as men, 'cause Christ wasn't a woman! Where did your Christ come from? Where did your Christ come from? From god and a woman! Man had nothing to do with him.

If the first woman God ever made was strong enough to turn the world upside down all alone, these women together ought to be able to turn it back, and get it right side up again! And now they is asking to do it, the men better let them. Obliged to you for hearing me, and now old Sojourner ain't got nothing more to say. ❖

© GREAT SOURCE. COPYING IS PROHIBITED.

✳ After your first reading, what do you think is the main idea of Sojourner Truth's speech?

_____

_____

_____

_____

✳ Now reread the speech so that you can summarize it. As you read, write the main ideas in the **Response Notes** and circle the details in the speech that support what you have written.

✳ Using your annotations, write a summary of Truth's speech. As a challenge, limit your summary to three sentences that contain all of the important points.

_____

_____

_____

_____

_____

_____

_____

_____

_____

_____

_____

_____

Writing a summary of a
selection helps you identify and
remember the key points.

© GREAT SOURCE. COPYING IS PROHIBITED.

If you are like most readers, you see pictures in your mind as you read. **Visualizing** is a way to understand what you are reading by using the author's words and your prior knowledge to make pictures in your mind.

If you read a story or poem about a person who is a lot like a friend, your mental picture will probably look quite a bit like your friend. If you are reading about a subject or person totally unfamiliar to you, your mental pictures will be formed by the words the author uses. Some students have said they see movies in their minds as they read. Being able to "see" what you are reading will help you become a better reader.

In this lesson, you are going to draw some of the pictures you form in your mind as you read about Mattie Stepanek. First, here is some information about Mattie. Use the **Response Notes** to record drawings or quick sketches that show what you are seeing in your mind as you read.

A REMARKABLE BOY

Mattie Stepanek was born with a rare form of muscular dystrophy. His mom, Jeni, also has the disease, which she didn't discover until after she had four children. Mattie's three siblings all died from the disease—but remarkably, Mattie recovered many times from near-fatal episodes. It was only in 2004 that his body was no longer able to survive his debilitating disease. Yet, he had achieved great feats: earning a junior black belt in martial arts, reaching the 11th grade level in home-schooling, and having his poetry published.

THREE WISHES

Mattie always had three wishes: to have his poems published, to meet his hero Jimmy Carter, and to share his message of peace on *The Oprah Winfrey Show*. All three of his wishes were granted. When Oprah asked Mattie why he had chosen those three wishes, he explained, "Because they were things that would last forever. Going to Disney World ends in a week. But being able to talk with Jimmy Carter, being able to have my books published, being able to talk to you here today, lasts forever."

© GREAT SOURCE. COPYING IS PROHIBITED.

✳ Compare your visual notes with a partner. What pictures did you
see? What is your impression of Mattie?

_____

_____

_____

_____

Mattie wrote about an important monument to fallen soldiers.
As you read his poem, jot notes about any connections you make
with the poem.

Vietnam War Memorial
by Mattie Stepanek

Response
Notes

A wall gives structure.
It can divide and block.
It can support and fortify.
It can be a place to display
Photos, writings, awards,
And memories.
But this is The Wall.
The Wall that gives structure
To the insane losses of a war.
The Wall that represents
A nation divided and blocked.
The Wall that supports too
Many broken hearts and bodies.
The Wall that fortifies the reality
Of dead lives among the living.
The Wall that reflects memories
Of what was, of what is,
Of what might have been,
In photos, in letters and poems,
In medals of honor and dedication,
And in teddy bears, and flowers,
And tears and tears and tears.

This is The Wall,
Born out of pain and anguish
And guilt,
That gives names to the children
Of grieving mothers and fathers
And to the spouses of widows
And to parents of wondering children.
This is The Wall
That echoes sadness and fear,
Yet whispers relief and hope.
This is The Wall.
May we be forever blessed by its
Structure and fortitude and support,
And may we be forever reminded
Of the eternal divisions of war. ❖

Mattie Stepanek
1990-2004

© GREAT SOURCE. COPYING IS PROHIBITED.

✳ In the space below, draw the Vietnam War Memorial as you see it from reading Mattie's poem.

✳ Below your drawing, write a sentence explaining your drawing.

_____

_____

_____

_____

_____

_____

_____

Making pictures in your mind as you read enriches your understanding by helping you focus on the ideas and details.

© GREAT SOURCE. COPYING IS PROHIBITED.

When you look into a mirror and see your reflection, you think about how you look. You reflect on your reflection!

In the same way, when you think about what you have read, you are **reflecting.** One way to become a stronger reader is to take time to reflect, not just to read the words and then rush to the next activity. Reflecting means slowing down a bit, taking time to think a little longer about what you are reading, and perhaps to write down ideas as they come to you.

Reread the poem in Lesson 9, "Vietnam War Memorial." In the **Response Notes,** add notes about *reflecting* whenever you pause to think about an idea in the poem. You may also indicate places where you use the reading strategies you have practiced in prior lessons: *predicting, questioning, summarizing, visualizing.*

✳ Write a short paragraph telling which reading strategies—*reflecting, predicting, questioning, summarizing,* and *visualizing*—you used to help you understand this poem.

_____

_____

_____

_____

_____

_____

_____

_____

REFLECTING ON REMARKABLE PEOPLE

In this unit, you read excerpts from a novel, a speech, and a poem. You gained insights into a fictional character, an important woman in American history, and a young boy who inspired millions of everyday people as well as notable people such as former President Carter and Oprah Winfrey. As you reflect on these three people, think about how each might be called "remarkable."

Use the questions on page 38 to prompt some ideas. Try to come up with some additional questions of your own.

© GREAT SOURCE. COPYING IS PROHIBITED.

- What makes a person remarkable?
- What does being famous have to do with being remarkable?
- Does a remarkable person have to do something significant?
- Can a person be remarkable even if no one else knows what he or she has done?
- In what ways can remarkable people have an impact on the world?

✳ Write a paragraph reflecting on why you think any one or two of the people listed below might be called *remarkable*. Use quotations from the passages to support your ideas.

- Parvana
- Sojourner Truth
- Mattie Stepanek

_____

_____

_____

_____

_____

_____

_____

_____

_____

_____

_____

_____

Reflecting on your reading gives you time to consider carefully not only the author's words but also the meanings they convey.

© GREAT SOURCE. COPYING IS PROHIBITED.

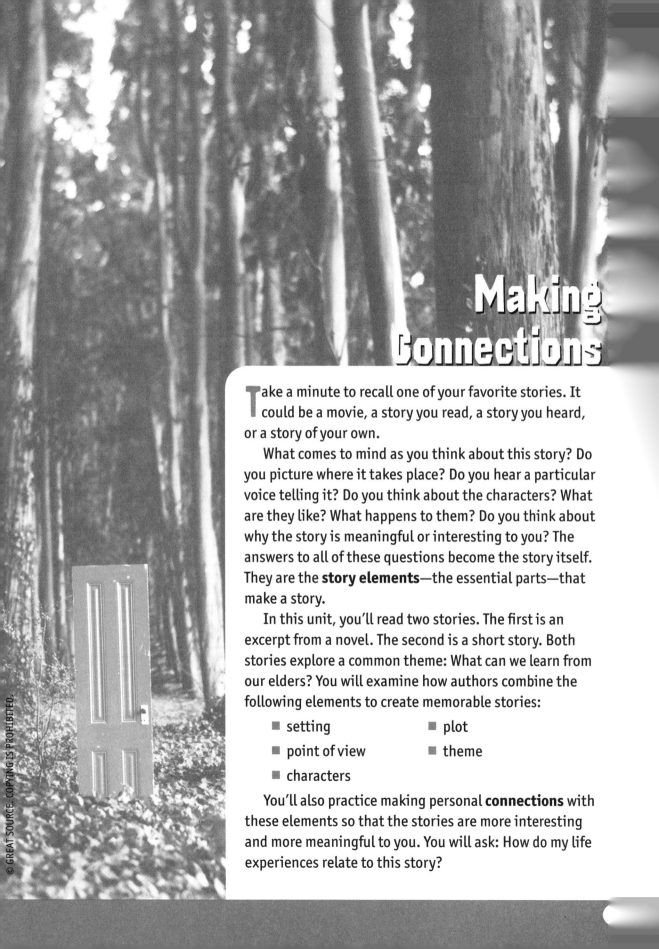

© GREAT SOURCE. COPYING IS PROHIBITED.

Making Connections

Take a minute to recall one of your favorite stories. It could be a movie, a story you read, a story you heard, or a story of your own.

What comes to mind as you think about this story? Do you picture where it takes place? Do you hear a particular voice telling it? Do you think about the characters? What are they like? What happens to them? Do you think about why the story is meaningful or interesting to you? The answers to all of these questions become the story itself. They are the **story elements**—the essential parts—that make a story.

In this unit, you'll read two stories. The first is an excerpt from a novel. The second is a short story. Both stories explore a common theme: What can we learn from our elders? You will examine how authors combine the following elements to create memorable stories:

- setting
- point of view
- characters
- plot
- theme

You'll also practice making personal **connections** with these elements so that the stories are more interesting and more meaningful to you. You will ask: How do my life experiences relate to this story?

T hink about the most interesting day of your life. If you told the story of that day to a friend, chances are you would include details about the **setting**—when and where the events and actions took place. Knowing the setting would help your friend understand the **context** of your story and picture it more vividly. That's how a setting works in any story. Descriptive details about when and where a story takes place help readers understand and picture the events.

The selection you will read is an excerpt from *Year of Impossible Goodbyes,* a novel by Sook Nyul Choi. It is set in northern Korea at the end of World War II. Concentrate on the images the author creates that help you **visualize** the setting. Circle descriptive words that help create your mental picture of the setting. Remember that setting has to do with both *when* and *where* the story takes place. In your **Response Notes,** write statements that tell both when and where the story takes place.

from **Year of Impossible Goodbyes** by Sook Nyul Choi

Response
Notes

Spring 1945
Small clusters of pale green needles emerged from the old weathered pine tree in our front yard. The high mounds of snow in the corner of our yard had begun to melt, the water flowing gently into the furrow of dark earth Grandfather had dug around the base of the tree like a moat. Grandfather's tree stood alone in the far corner of the yard, its dark green-needled branches emanating harmoniously from the trunk, reaching out like a large umbrella. It was a magic tree, holding in the shade of its branches the peace and harmony Grandfather so often talked about.

Despite the warmth of the sun, the air in Kirimni, Pyongyang, was dark and heavy, filled with the (sound of gunfire) and with the menacing glint of drawn (swords.) For the people in Kirimni, this day was no different from the bitter gray days of winter. The warmth of the spring sun and the thawing of the icy snow brought no respite from the oppressiveness that engulfed us.

Evidence of war

Grandfather, hoping the Korean people might experience the exhilaration and beauty of spring again, had made sure my mother included the word *chun,* or spring, in the names of each of my brothers. My oldest brother's name was Hanchun, meaning "Korean spring"; my second brother, Jaechun, was called "spring again"; my third brother, Hyunchun, the "wise spring"; and my youngest brother, Inchun, the "benevolent spring." Inchun was now almost seven, and a benevolent spring still had not come to our village. ❖

© GREAT SOURCE. COPYING IS PROHIBITED.

✻ Write a few sentences that describe the mental picture in your mind evoked by the author's descriptions.

_____

_____

_____

_____

✻ Compare your notes to a partner's. Discuss how your mental pictures are similar or different.

✻ When the setting of a story reminds you of another setting you are familiar with—an illustration or painting, a place you've been to, the setting of a movie you've seen, or the setting in another book—you can often picture it more vividly. Try to discover your own connections to the setting in the excerpt above. Fill in the Connections Chart below. Working with a partner may help you generate more ideas.

CONNECTIONS CHART

The setting from a movie or other book, place I've been to, or image I've seen . . .	. . . helps me to picture or understand this part of the selection better

Making connections to the setting of a story can help you visualize the time and place, which help you better understand the story.

© GREAT SOURCE. COPYING IS PROHIBITED.

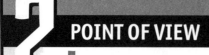
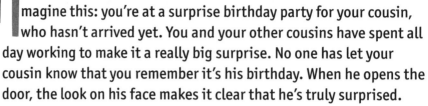

magine this: you're at a surprise birthday party for your cousin, who hasn't arrived yet. You and your other cousins have spent all day working to make it a really big surprise. No one has let your cousin know that you remember it's his birthday. When he opens the door, the look on his face makes it clear that he's truly surprised.

If you narrated—or told—the story of that day, it would definitely be different than if your cousin narrated it. **Point of view** has to do with the vantage point from which a story is told. It reveals who tells the story and what that narrator can "see"—in other words, how the narrator or the characters "see" the story. There are several possible points of view:

- **First-person point of view** When the narrator is one of the characters and calls himself or herself "I." This point of view often helps readers identify with the narrator.

- **Second-person point of view** When the story is written as if the reader is one of the characters and is the "you" referred to in the story.

- **Third-person point of view** When the narrator is a story-teller who isn't part of the story.

  * A *limited* third-person narrator reveals the thoughts and feelings of only one character. It's as if the storyteller is perched on one character's shoulders and can see inside that character's head.

  * An *omniscient* (all-knowing) third-person narrator reveals the thoughts and feelings of several characters. It's as if the storyteller can fly around, seeing what goes on everywhere, and looking into several characters' minds.

Read another excerpt from *Year of Impossible Goodbyes*. In your **Response Notes,** jot down everything you learn about the narrator.

from **Year of Impossible Goodbyes**
by Sook Nyul Choi

I saw Grandfather peer out at the yard from his room, and look at the delicate branches of the pine tree playing against the hazy, pale blue sky. He cleared his throat and called out to Mother. "Hyunsuk, today I will do my morning meditation under the tree."

© GREAT SOURCE. COPYING IS PROHIBITED.

"It is not all of a sudden. Not a single day has gone by that I haven't thought of it. It has been thirty-six years since I have meditated in the warmth of a spring sun. Today, the Japanese soldiers will not keep me inside. I am too old and too tired to be afraid anymore."

Although Mother let out a heavy sigh, she did not protest. Reluctantly, she brought out a clean straw mat and unrolled it beneath the pine tree, placing the thick cushion in the center of the shade. Grandfather emerged from his room and became part of the peaceful scene. The gentle rays of the April sun flitting through the pine branches played upon his face like dancing fairies.

Excited to see Grandfather meditate beneath his tree, I slid my rice-paper door open a crack and watched. ❖

✳ **What do you want to know that you can't learn from the narrator's vantage point? What other points of view are possible besides the narrator's? Write what you would like to know more about.**

_____

_____

_____

_____

_____

_____

_____

_____

_____

✳ **Get together with a partner and discuss what each of you would like to know more about.**

✳ **On page 44 is another excerpt from the novel. In your Response Notes jot anything you learn about the narrator and the grandfather.**

© GREAT SOURCE. COPYING IS PROHIBITED.

from **Year of Impossible Goodbyes** by Sook Nyul Choi

. . . I crossed my legs, resting my hands on my lap with the palms facing up, just as he did. Though his eyes were closed, I kept mine open to watch him. He sat tall and still, like a statue. He looked peaceful as he prayed, yet there was an intensity, an anticipation, in his expression, as though he were waiting for something special to happen. His wrinkles were deep, and I wished that I could run my fingers along the creases in his forehead as he sat motionless in prayer. I wondered what he had to tell the Buddha this morning.

He was still for so long. I began to worry that my Grandfather had been filled with the spirit of the Buddha and had been turned into a statue. I tiptoed outside, quietly crept up toward him, and put my finger under his nose. I felt his faint breath and he coughed gently to reassure me. I sat next to him and watched, happy to be near him. The smell of the pine permeated the atmosphere, and I breathed deeply.

The sun grew stronger as I watched Grandfather, whose shirt of worn gray cloth hung comfortably from his bony shoulders. His crossed legs looked like two bent chopsticks. His handsome face was sad, peaceful, intent, but always dignified.

. . . Grandfather opened his eyes and looked at me as if he knew I had been staring at him. I was disappointed to see him stir; time would no longer stand still. He looked deep into my eyes, and then smiled, happy that we had celebrated this spring day together in such a special way. We got up and hurried inside to start our morning lessons. ❖

✳ In the excerpt, the narrator wonders what is going on in her grandfather's mind. Become the narrator of this story, using a third-person limited point-of-view. Perch on grandfather's shoulders and narrate on the writing lines what you imagine is going on in his mind.

_____

_____

_____

_____

_____

_____

The point of view from which a story is told determines the limits on the type of information or insights that will be revealed.

© GREAT SOURCE. COPYING IS PROHIBITED.

As in a play, a story is populated by a cast of characters. Authors use a range of techniques to reveal details about their story's cast. The way that authors reveal information about their characters is referred to as **characterization.** Some common techniques that reveal a character's personality are the following:

- the narrator's direct descriptions
- the character's words, thoughts, and actions
- other characters' words or thoughts

Characterization allows the people in stories to come alive, enabling us to relate to and interact with them.

Think about the characters you have met in stories. Can you think of characters you could relate to? Ones who have reminded you of someone? Ones you have learned from? Characters you liked? Others you didn't? Often, it is the characters in a story that make it memorable. Making personal connections with characters—connecting them to ourselves, to people we know, or to other characters—makes stories more meaningful.

As you read the first part of the following short story, mark in the text examples of the specific characterization techniques listed above. Record in your **Response Notes** any connections you make with the character. An example is done for you.

"Thank You, Ma'm" by Langston Hughes

© GREAT SOURCE. COPYING IS PROHIBITED.

She was a large woman with a large purse that had everything in it but hammer and nails. It had a long strap, and she carried it slung across her shoulder. It was about eleven o'clock at night, dark, and she was walking alone, when a boy ran up behind her and tried to snatch her purse. The strap broke with the single tug the boy gave it from behind. But the boy's weight and the weight of the purse combined caused him to lose his balance. Instead of taking off full blast as he had hoped, the boy fell on his back on the sidewalk and his legs flew up. The large woman simply turned around and kicked him right square in his blue-jeaned sitter. Then she reached down, picked the boy up by his shirt front, and shook him until his teeth rattled.

After that the woman said, "Pick up my pocketbook, boy, and give it here."

She still held him tightly. But she bent down enough to permit him to stoop and pick up her purse. Then she said, "Now ain't you ashamed of yourself?"

Response Notes

Narrator's description makes her seem big and tougher than she might really look.

Firmly gripped by his shirt front, the boy said, "Yes'm."

The woman said, "What did you want to do it for?"

The boy said, "I didn't aim to."

She said, "You a lie!"

"If I turn you loose, will you run?" asked the woman.

"Yes'm," said the boy.

"Then I won't turn you loose," said the woman. She did not release him.

"Lady, I'm sorry," whispered the boy.

"Um-hum! Your face is dirty. I got a great mind to wash your face for you. Ain't you got nobody home to tell you to wash your face?"

"No'm," said the boy.

"Then it will get washed this evening," said the large woman, starting up the street, dragging the frightened boy behind her.

He looked as if he were fourteen or fifteen, frail and willow-wild, in tennis shoes and blue jeans.

The woman said, "You ought to be my son. I would teach you right from wrong. Least I can do right now is to wash your face. Are you hungry?"

"No'm," said the being-dragged boy. "I just want you to turn me loose."

"Was I bothering *you* when I turned that corner?" asked the woman.

"No'm."

"But you put yourself in contact with me," said the woman. "If you think that that contact is not going to last awhile, you got another thought coming. When I get through with you, sir, you are going to remember Mrs. Luella Bates Washington Jones."

Sweat popped out on the boy's face and he began to struggle. Mrs. Jones stopped, jerked him around in front of her, put a half-nelson about his neck, and continued to drag him up the street. When she got to her door, she dragged the boy inside, down a hall, and into a large kitchenette-furnished room at the rear of the house. She switched on the light and left the door open. The boy could hear other roomers laughing and talking in the large house. Some of their doors were open, too, so he knew he and the woman were not alone. The woman still had him by the neck in the middle of her room.

She said, "What is your name?"

"Roger," answered the boy.

"Then, Roger, you go to that sink and wash your face," said the woman, whereupon she turned him loose at last. Roger looked at the door—looked at the woman—looked at the door—*and went to the sink.* ❖

© GREAT SOURCE. COPYING IS PROHIBITED.

✳ Take a moment to look over your **Response Notes.** Compare what you wrote with a partner's notes. Help each other decide the strongest connections you made with each of the characters.

✳ Write a character sketch that describes the qualities of the character you most strongly connect to. Is it Roger or Mrs. Jones? Explain why you made this connection.

_____

_____

_____

_____

_____

_____

_____

_____

_____

_____

_____

_____

_____

_____

_____

_____

✳ How does this connection contribute to your understanding and response to the characters in the story?

_____

_____

_____

_____

_____

_____

Making connections to characters can enhance your understanding and strengthen your response to their viewpoints and actions.

© GREAT SOURCE. COPYING IS PROHIBITED.

14 PLOT

Think back to the example of the birthday party described in Lesson 12. If you were to tell the story of that day, what events would you choose to share? Certainly you wouldn't tell *everything* that happened that day. Instead, you would choose interesting, important, or relevant events. An author has to make similar decisions to create the **plot** of a compelling story. Each event is carefully chosen to work with the other events.

Recall the first part of "Thank You, Ma'm" as you read the rest of the story. In the **Response Notes,** summarize plot events as you read. An example is done for you.

Response Notes

Roger washes his face as he tells Mrs. Jones why he tried to steal her pocketbook.

"Thank You, Ma'm" by Langston Hughes *(continued)*

"Let the water run until it gets warm," she said. "Here's a clean towel."

"You gonna take me to jail?" asked the boy, bending over the sink.

"Not with that face, I would not take you nowhere," said the woman. "Here I am trying to get home to cook me a bite to eat and you snatch my pocketbook! Maybe, you ain't been to your supper either, late as it be. Have you?"

"There's nobody home at my house," said the boy.

"Then we'll eat," said the woman, "I believe you're hungry—or been hungry—to try to snatch my pocketbook."

"I want a pair of blue suede shoes," said the boy.

"Well, you didn't have to snatch *my* pocketbook to get some suede shoes," said Mrs. Luella Bates Washington Jones. "You could of asked me."

"Ma'm?"

The water dripping from his face, the boy looked at her. There was a long pause. A very long pause. After he had dried his face and not knowing what else to do, dried it again, the boy turned around, wondering what next. The door was open. He could make a dash for it down the hall. He could run, run, run, *run!*

The woman was sitting on the day-bed. After a while she said, "I were young once and I wanted things I could not get."

There was another long pause. The boy's mouth opened. Then he frowned, but not knowing he frowned.

The woman said, "Um-hum! You thought I was going to say *but,* didn't you? You thought I was going to say, *but I didn't snatch people's pocketbooks.* Well, I wasn't going to say that." Pause. Silence. "I have done things, too, which I would not tell you, son—neither tell God, if he didn't already know. Everybody's got

© GREAT SOURCE. COPYING IS PROHIBITED.

something in common. So you set down while I fix us something to eat. You might run that comb through your hair so you will look presentable."

In another corner of the room behind a screen was a gas plate and an ice-box. Mrs. Jones got up and went behind the screen. The woman did not watch the boy to see if he was going to run now, nor did she watch her purse which she left behind her on the day-bed. But the boy took care to sit on the far side of the room where he thought she could easily see him out of the corner of her eye, if she wanted to. He did not trust the woman *not* to trust him. And he did not want to be mistrusted now.

"Do you need somebody to go to the store," asked the boy, "maybe to get some milk or something?"

"Don't believe I do," said the woman, "unless you just want sweet milk yourself. I was going to make cocoa out of this canned milk I got here."

"That will be fine," said the boy.

She heated some lima beans and ham she had in the icebox, made the cocoa, and set the table. The woman did not ask the boy anything about where he lived, or his folks, or anything else that would embarrass him. Instead, as they ate, she told him about her job in a hotel beauty-shop that stayed open late, what the work was like, and how all kinds of women came in and out, blondes, red-heads, and Spanish. Then she cut him a half of her ten-cent cake.

"Eat some more, son," she said.

When they were finished eating she got up and said, "Now, here, take this ten dollars and buy yourself some blue suede shoes. And next time, do not make the mistake of latching onto *my* pocketbook *nor nobody else's*—because shoes got by devilish ways will burn your feet. I got to get my rest now. But from here on in, son, I hope you will behave yourself."

She led him down the hall to the front door and opened it. "Good-night! Behave yourself, boy!" she said, looking out into the street as he went down the steps.

The boy wanted to say something else other than, "Thank you, Ma'm," to Mrs. Luella Bates Washington Jones, but although his lips moved, he couldn't even say that as he turned at the foot of the barren stoop and looked up at the large woman in the door. Then she shut the door. ❖

© GREAT SOURCE. COPYING IS PROHIBITED.

✳ Look over your **Response Notes** for the whole story (beginning with Lesson 13) and consider the events Hughes chose as he wrote the story. List them in the space provided.

1. _____   2. _____

3. _____   4. _____

5. _____   6. _____

✳ Share your list with a partner and compare the events each of you chose. Why is each event important? What does each event tell us about the characters?

✳ At any point while you were reading "Thank You, Ma'm," did you find yourself thinking, "Hey! That reminds me of a time when . . ." or "Oh, that's kind of similar to what happened in . . ."? If you did, you made a connection with the plot of the story. Talk with a partner or a group about connections you made with the story.

✳ Think about one connection you made with the events of "Thank You, Ma'm." Use it to fill in the Connection Chart below.

CONNECTION CHART

This part of the plot of "Thank You, Ma'm"	. . . connects to this

✳ How does this connection influence your understanding of the story? How does it influence your response?

_____

_____

_____

Identifying the plot helps you to understand and make connections with stories.

_____

_____

_____

© GREAT SOURCE. COPYING IS PROHIBITED.

Stories play an important role in our lives. In addition to entertaining, they often prompt us to think about new things or to think about things in new ways. They sometimes teach us lessons, and they frequently help us understand others and ourselves better.

A **theme** is the main topic or message that is explored through the characters and the plot. Most stories have several themes. Some stories have clear messages, while others simply illuminate or explore topics. One way, then, to describe a theme is as a "topic *plus*." For example, the topic of a text could be "growing up." Ask yourself, what does the text *say* about growing up? The answer could be that the theme is "the struggles of growing up" or that "positive role models are important for teenagers." To understand a story's theme, ask: What does this author lead me to think about or understand?

One common theme in *Year of Impossible Goodbyes* and "Thank You, Ma'm" is *what we can learn from our elders*. What do you think each selection says about what we can learn from people older than ourselves? Fill in the Theme Chart below with your response. Include evidence from the text to support what you say.

THEME CHART

What Sookan learns from her grandfather in *Year of Impossible Goodbyes*
Evidence from story that makes me think so
What Roger learns from Mrs. Luella Bates Washington Jones in "Thank You, Ma'm"
Evidence from story that makes me think so

© GREAT SOURCE. COPYING IS PROHIBITED.

✳ Write a short essay describing how the stories *Year of Impossible Goodbyes* and "Thank You, Ma'm" help you think about what you can learn from your elders. Use your Theme Chart to provide specifics.

Title: _____

_____

_____

_____

_____

_____

_____

_____

_____

_____

_____

_____

_____

_____

✳ Make a personal connection with the theme you explored in your essay. Does it relate to anything in your own life? To the life of someone you know? Or does it relate to the theme in another text you're familiar with? Explain the connection.

_____

_____

_____

_____

_____

_____

Identifying and making personal connections with themes deepens your understanding of a story.

© GREAT SOURCE. COPYING IS PROHIBITED.

Exploring Multiple Perspectives

"A life is not important except in the impact it has on other lives."

—*Jackie Robinson*

When you hear the name "Jackie Robinson," whom do you picture? A gifted athlete who excelled in sports as varied as baseball, tennis, football, and golf? The first African American to play major league baseball? A man devoted to his family? A tireless worker for civil rights? Those are all aspects of Jackie Robinson.

In this unit, you will explore different views, or **perspectives,** of this famous man. No single text can reveal everything about Jackie Robinson, but each one will add insight to the overall picture. You will also learn that *who* tells the story has a lot to do with *what* the story says.

© GREAT SOURCE. COPYING IS PROHIBITED.

Interpretation—everyone does it. We take the facts as we know them and, in writing them, add our own understanding. A biographer examines the facts of a person's life. Some biographers try to present an impartial view by focusing only on the facts. Others reveal their feelings about the subject in the way they select and interpret the facts. They may include facts that make the person look better or worse than he or she really was. Or a writer might select only the incidents from a person's life that illustrate a certain point.

Robert Peterson combines facts and his own commentary, or interpretation, in "Hero on the Ball Field." As you read, use a highlighter of one color to mark the places where Peterson **draws conclusions,** such as "It was a tough time to be black, and not just for baseball players." Use a highlighter of a different color to mark the **facts,** such as "In Southern states, black kids went to separate schools."

"Hero on the Ball Field" by Robert Peterson

Response Notes

As a baseball player, Jackie Robinson won over the fans, his teammates—and his own hot temper.

Robinson was a line-drive hitter, an acrobatic fielder and the best base runner of his time. He was also the first African- American player in the big leagues in [the last] century.

In Robinson's rookie year, 1947, baseball topped the sports world. Pro football and basketball were far less popular 50 years ago.

It was a tough time to be black, and not just for baseball players. In Southern states, black kids went to separate schools. Black people had to ride in the backs of buses. There were even separate drinking fountains for blacks and whites. In the North, things were a little better, but not much. There had not been a black player in the major leagues in more than 60 years.

Blacks—even those good enough to play major-league baseball—had their own teams and leagues.

Jackie Robinson was a fiery competitor. "This guy didn't just come to play," an old baseball man once said. "He came to beat you!"

When the Brooklyn Dodgers signed Robinson, the club president, Branch Rickey, told Robinson he would have to curb his temper if he was abused or taunted by white players or fans. Rickey worried that if Robinson answered back, people who did not want blacks in baseball would say, "See, we told you blacks and whites should not compete."

Robinson asked, "Mr. Rickey, do you want a player who's afraid to fight back?"

© GREAT SOURCE. COPYING IS PROHIBITED.

"I want a player with guts enough not to fight back," Rickey said. "You've got to do this job with base hits and stolen bases and fielding ground balls, Jackie. Nothing else."

Jackie Robinson was the loneliest man in baseball in 1947. During spring training a half-dozen Dodgers players said they would not play if he joined the team. Branch Rickey put down that mutiny with stern words. Soon most Dodgers warmed up to Robinson. They saw he was helping them win games.

Opponents were not so friendly. Some made it as tough as they could for the black pioneer. A few tried to spike Robinson as they crossed first base, Robinson's position that year, on a close play. He was hit by pitches nine times. Once he was kicked as he slid into second base.

Many players and fans screamed racial taunts at him.

"Plenty of times I wanted to haul off when somebody insulted me for the color of my skin," he said later.

Robinson was not even safe from hate at home. The mail brought letters threatening his life. Some letter writers said they would kidnap his infant son, Jackie Jr., or attack his wife.

Despite the great pressure on him, Robinson had a fine season. He batted .297, led the Dodgers in runs scored with 125 and hit 12 home runs. He led the league with 29 stolen bases. That may not seem like a lot today, but baseball was not a running game in 1947.

As a base runner, Robinson was constantly in motion. Pitchers worried more about him than the batter. Often the batter got a fat pitch to hit because the dancing Robinson distracted the pitcher.

Robinson sometimes "stole" bases after the ball was hit. He would race from first to third when the safe thing to do was stop at second.

But here is a fact that tells you how daring the muscular, pigeon-toed Robinson was on the bases: He stole home 19 times in his career, more than anyone since the early years of this century.

Fans—black and white—flocked to see Jackie Robinson play. In his first year, the Dodgers and four other National League teams set attendance records. He became a hero in black communities.

That year the Dodgers won the National League pennant but lost the World Series to the New York Yankees. Robinson was named National League Rookie of the Year.

Even before the 1947 season ended, Robinson's success paved the way for other black players. In July the Cleveland Indians signed Larry Doby, a slugging young outfielder, who became the first black player in the American League. A month later, pitcher Dan Bankhead, who had been with the Memphis Red Sox in the Negro American League, joined Robinson on the Dodgers.

Jackie Robinson's best position was second base, but he played all four infield positions and some in the outfield.

© GREAT SOURCE. COPYING IS PROHIBITED.

SEC. 23

From 1949 to 1952 he was one of the two or three best players in base-ball. In 1949 he led the National League in batting with a .342 average and in stolen bases with 37. He was third in triples and runs scored. That performance earned him the league's Most Valuable Player award.

Robinson retired from baseball in 1957, the year before the Dodgers moved to Los Angeles. Five years later he was elected to the Baseball Hall of Fame.

He became an outspoken leader in the fight for equality for black people. Jackie Robinson proved himself a hero off the baseball field as well as on. ❖

※ **Does Peterson use more facts or more commentary? Why do you think he wrote Robinson's biography this way?**

_____

_____

_____

_____

_____

_____

_____

_____

※ **Look back at the commentary you highlighted. What does Robert Peterson think of Jackie Robinson? How can you tell?**

_____

_____

_____

_____

_____

_____

_____

© GREAT SOURCE. COPYING IS PROHIBITED.

✳ Fill out the chart below to help you understand how Peterson
uses incidents to express his perspective on Jackie Robinson.

Incident	What the incident reveals about Robinson
Robinson receives hate mail	Robinson was able to perform well even under intense pressure and stress.

Biographers often select and present facts about a person that reveal the biographer's point of view about that person.

© GREAT SOURCE. COPYING IS PROHIBITED.

In reading or listening to an **interview,** we get information and impressions about a person. The information is filtered through the people participating in the interview, though. The questions the interviewer asks will determine the information the interviewee gives. The interviewee will put his or her own interpretations on the facts, based on previous experiences.

In 1997, Bryan Ethier interviewed Henry "Hank" Aaron about Jackie Robinson. Aaron himself was famous. When the Atlanta Braves player hit home run 715 on April 8, 1974, Aaron shattered Babe Ruth's 39-year record. Although many people applauded this accomplishment, others were upset that a black man had broken a white man's record. According to Ethier, Aaron received death threats and "had even feared for his children's safety. But through it all, Aaron had kept his emotions to himself, letting his bat do his talking; it was a policy he had followed throughout his career."

As you read, think about what Aaron reveals about Jackie Robinson. In the **Response Notes,** mark the places where you learn something about Robinson's influence and his personal qualities.

from "**Henry Aaron Remembers**" by Bryan Ethier

Response Notes

AMERICAN HISTORY [the name of the magazine in which the interview was published]**:** As a young black ballplayer, what was your reaction when you learned of Jackie Robinson signing with the Dodgers?

HENRY AARON: Well, I guess it was kind of like putting it in the same perspective as the signing of the bill that ended discrimination as far as drinking fountains and railroads and bath facilities, and things like that. Kind of taking a burden off your back, when you felt like Jackie Robinson had done something to give every black kid a chance to live his dream.

AH: Do you recall the time, as a young player, when you first met Jackie?

AARON: When I was in high school—when I was in Mobile, Alabama—I remember Jackie Robinson. They had a farm team in Mobile, and teams always used to come through there to play the Mobile Bears. And Jackie came there to make a speech, and I remember that I stayed out of school to listen to him speak.

AH: Did that speech, and meeting him at that time, set your career on its course?

AARON: Well, he certainly did affect me when I listened to him. But even before then he affected me, just knowing that Jackie Robinson was the

© GREAT SOURCE. COPYING IS PROHIBITED.

first black man that ever played professional baseball certainly inspired me to go ahead and fulfill my dream.

• • •

AH: There was some comment at the time that Jackie was brought up by Branch Rickey more because of his personality, his upbringing, and his intelligence than for his baseball ability. Perhaps there were more athletic players who could have been brought up?

AARON: I'm sure some of that was true. I'm sure they probably could've brought in a lot more, many more, players that had more talent than Jackie Robinson. But that wasn't the only criteria at that time. You had to have somebody who could deal with the pressure; you had to have somebody who had the outlook of a Dr. Martin Luther King, who could turn the other cheek at times, and also be able to play baseball so that people would appreciate it. So, I'm sure the things mentioned, all of that was true.

• • •

AH: Over his career, Jackie began to change and became more embittered, did he not?

AARON: He had proven himself, that if given the opportunity he could play baseball. He had proven that to himself, but he was a man, and he had a temper just like everyone else. He felt like he had done all of these things, and he just needed to be his own man. He had a lot of pressure stored up in him from when people would slide into him, slap him, call him names, and all that other stuff. He just felt like he didn't need to take that anymore. ❖

※ What is your first reaction to this interview? Jot down a few notes about your impressions of Jackie Robinson and Hank Aaron.

_____

_____

_____

※ Explain how Aaron answers the reporter's questions about Robinson's playing ability and about Robinson becoming embittered. How does Aaron stress the positive side of Robinson?

_____

_____

_____

_____

_____

© GREAT SOURCE. COPYING IS PROHIBITED.

✳ Think of a famous person. Write three questions that you could ask someone about that person.

Name of Person _____

_____
_____
_____

✳ Now imagine two different interviews. The first one will be with someone who admires the person. The second one will be with someone who does not. Organize your questions and answers below.

Famous Person _____

Interview with person who admires him/her

Q _____
A _____
_____

Q _____
A _____
_____

Q _____
A _____
_____

Interview with person who does not admire him/her

Q (same as above) _____
A _____
_____

Q _____
A _____
_____

Q _____
A _____

© GREAT SOURCE. COPYING IS PROHIBITED.

✳ Look at the introduction to "Henry Aaron Remembers." Review what you marked in the **Response Notes,** and re-read the excerpt from *Hero on the Ballfield* in Lesson 16. Use a Venn diagram to compare these two views of Jackie Robinson.

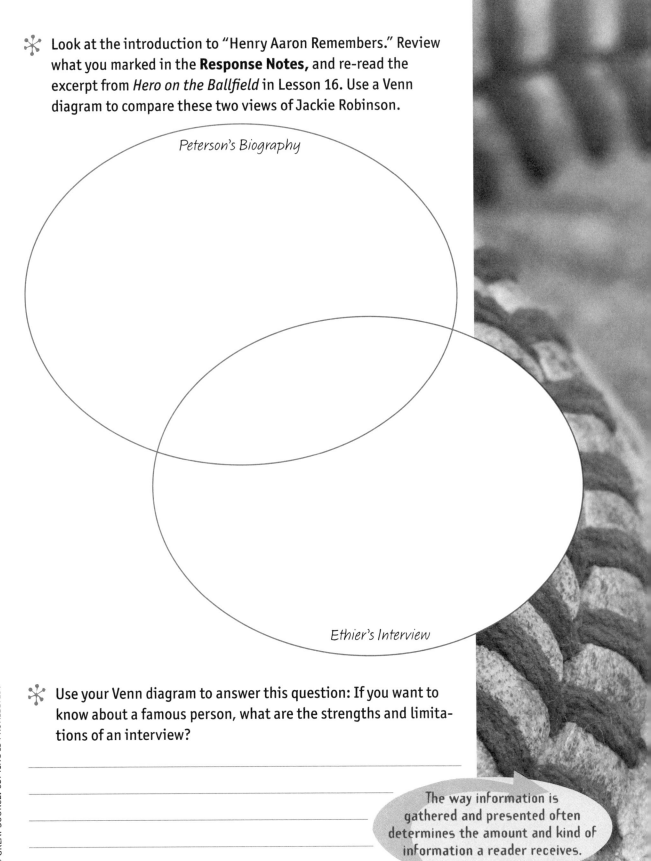

Peterson's Biography

Ethier's Interview

✳ Use your Venn diagram to answer this question: If you want to know about a famous person, what are the strengths and limitations of an interview?

_____

_____

_____

_____

_____

The way information is gathered and presented often determines the amount and kind of information a reader receives.

© GREAT SOURCE. COPYING IS PROHIBITED.

Another perspective on a person's life can come from someone close to that person—a relative or good friend. Sharon Robinson, Jackie's daughter, has a perspective that allows her to know some details that a biographer with an outside perspective might not. However, as a family member, her depiction of her father will undoubtedly be filtered through her thoughts about and feelings for him.

In her **autobiography,** *Stealing Home,* Sharon Robinson tells about her childhood in a famous family. In this excerpt, she recounts a dinner-table conversation. Jackie Robinson is talking about an incident in Little Rock, Arkansas, in 1957. When nine black teenagers began the court-ordered integration of schools, they faced jeers, taunts, and humiliation. Four of the children had spoken with Robinson about the ordeal. As you read this personal account, mark places where Sharon Robinson reveals her own thoughts.

Response Notes

from **Stealing Home** by Sharon Robinson

Without talking down to us, Dad used this opportunity to explain prejudice. Generally, he moved quietly around the house, but it was obvious that this situation had him worked up and he wanted my brothers and me to understand the situation.

"I suppose we all fear the unknown—the strange, the different. The natural fears of parents are made worse by ignorance, and unfortunately they pass them down to their children. In the process, the stories get more and more distorted and eventually become fact in the minds of the storyteller. The sad part for everyone is that prejudice prevents people from sharing talents which could benefit the whole community. The only way racial discrimination can have a hope of being erased is through exposure. The more people understand each other the less they will fear the differences."

"What did you say to the children, Daddy?" I asked, trying to picture their faces.

"Were they boys or girls?" David added.

"How old were they?" Jackie wanted to know.

Dad smiled and continued with the story of his phone conversation. He reminded us that the boys and girls were high school students. I felt somewhat relieved to know that they were much older than we were. I wondered how the children could possibly learn under such tremendous pressure.

I looked questioningly at Jackie, who was ten at the time, trying to picture him as a teenager going to high school. I figured my rebellious brother, Jackie

© GREAT SOURCE. COPYING IS PROHIBITED.

Junior, would arrive at school and when he was told he couldn't go inside, he would drop his books right in front of the soldiers (because he'd have to do something defiant), turn around, and go to the movies with his friends. I started to laugh at that image but then the sound of Dad's voice reminded me that we were discussing something serious. I took another bite of the baked chicken on my plate and chewed it, quietly listening to Dad.

"One of the girls I talked to this morning was named Gloria Ray and another was Minnie Brown. I told the girls that they were doing a tremendous job that made us swell up with pride. I wanted them to know that there were people throughout the country supporting them," Dad went on. "I couldn't believe Minnie's response. She said that they were following in my footsteps. Can you imagine?"

Dad's voice had faded. I had to strain to hear him. He was staring straight ahead not really focused on any one person, but I could still see the tears building in his eyes. I watched as he blinked several times. His expression said more than his words: a sadness because the children were so young; a pride in their courage and determination. I am sure that he also felt good playing a role, and grateful that the school experiences of his own children did not include such extreme displays of hatred.

I went to bed that night and dreamed of linking arms with Gloria, Minnie, Thelma, and Melba. We formed an impenetrable barrier. Our faces conveyed an unstoppable message. The National Guard offered no resistance. They parted their ranks and we entered Central High School. As far away as Arkansas was from Connecticut, I felt a bond with the children in Little Rock. ❖

✳ How would you describe Sharon Robinson's attitude toward her father in this excerpt? Write two quotations that support your description.

_____

_____

_____

_____

_____

_____

_____

_____

_____

© GREAT SOURCE. COPYING IS PROHIBITED.

✳ You have read three different pieces of writing about Jackie Robinson. Brainstorm a list of Robinson's personal characteristics based on what you have learned from these pieces of writing. Then identify the source or sources for each characteristic by marking it B (Biography), I (Interview), or PA (Personal Account).

✳ Imagine that a friend wants to learn more about Jackie Robinson and has asked you to recommend a resource. You might not have a specific title in mind, but what kind of writing would you tell your friend to look for? Which perspective would you recommend that your friend begin with and why?

_____

_____

_____

_____

_____

_____

_____

A personal account or memoir can provide readers with insights and details that may be absent from accounts with a more distant perspective.

© GREAT SOURCE. COPYING IS PROHIBITED.

A poet can provide another perspective on a person. Although this poem doesn't provide information about Jackie Robinson, it does give you another way to think about him. It adds another perspective to consider as you create an image of Jackie Robinson.

In a few lines, Lucille Clifton uses **powerful images** to portray Jackie Robinson. Her impression of him becomes clearer each time you read the poem. Read it two or three times, each time adding questions or insights to your **Response Notes.** Mark the images that strike you.

jackie robinson by Lucille Clifton

Response
Notes

> ran against walls
> without breaking.
> in night games
> was not foul
> but, brave as a hit
> over whitestone fences,
> entered the conquering dark. ❖

❊ Lucille Clifton's language in this poem is distilled to present the essence of Jackie Robinson as she sees him. If the poem seems too condensed, try this: Rewrite the poem as two sentences, each starting with "Jackie Robinson" and ending with the periods that are already in the poem.

_____

_____

_____

_____

❊ What characteristics of Robinson does Clifton emphasize?

_____

_____

_____

© GREAT SOURCE. COPYING IS PRHIBITED.

✴ Try your hand at using Clifton's poetic style. Choose a famous person. Use Clifton's poem as a model for a poem you will write. Use the line beneath each of her lines to help you follow her word pattern in your poem.

ran against walls

_____

without breaking.

_____

in night games

_____

was not foul

_____

but, brave as a hit

_____

over whitestone fences,

_____

entered the conquering dark.

_____

Poetic images can provide an impressionistic and emotional perspective of a person.

COPYING IS PROHIBITED.

One incident can reveal much about a person. Nan Birmingham briefly met Jackie Robinson when she sat next to him on an airplane in the late 1960s. He had been retired since 1957, but he was still well known. As you read Ms. Birmingham's story, think about how your impression of Jackie Robinson is enhanced or changed.

"Lady, That's Jackie Robinson!" by Nan Birmingham

Response Notes

I was bone-tired by 2 a.m., when I boarded the plane for home after criss-crossing six southern states in five days on the lecture circuit. Gradually, I became aware that passengers shuffling with fatigue along the aisle perked up when they passed the man seated next to me.

"I should be asleep at home by now," he said quietly. "I only flew south for dinner." "Dinner?" I asked, searching for clues to his identity. "I was the speaker at the National Conference of Christians and Jews," he explained. I wrestled with famous names and came up empty.

Before dawn the PA [on the airplane] announced that Kennedy was again socked in. We were to land in Newark and be bused to JFK. My seatmate gave in to annoyance. "I still have to drive to Connecticut."

"Do you take the thruway?" I asked. "I live in Westchester just off the thruway. You wouldn't have to stop. Just slow down. I'll jump."

"You wouldn't have to do that," he said with a smile.

When he left his seat briefly, the man across the aisle whispered, "What a great guy is giving you a ride."

"Yes," I agreed knowingly. Then I chanced, "He is Elston Howard, isn't he?"

"Elston Howard?" the fellow bellowed. "Lady, *that's* Jackie Robinson!" he added in utter amazement.

Jackie Robinson refastened his seatbelt. I wanted him to know I knew and exploded enthusiastically. "My sister, Marion, was at UCLA when you played for the Bruins."

"Really," he said calmly. "That was some time ago. I'm Jackie Robinson, and what is your name?"

When the bus pulled up at Kennedy on that gray morning, Jackie Robinson stood up in front and shouted, "If anyone needs a ride to Westchester or Connecticut, I'm driving up the New England Thruway."

A young soldier spoke up, "Sir, I'm going to Waterbury."

"Come along," said Robinson.

As the soldier and I waited for Robinson to come with his car I said with a certain know-it-all smugness, "Young man, are you aware of just *who* is giving us a ride?"

© GREAT SOURCE. COPYING IS PRHIBITED.

"Man, am I!" he beamed. "I can't wait to tell my mama. She's in the hospital. This is going to make her feel real good."

The morning light and exhaustion stripped away pretense, and we spoke candidly about our families and children as the car nosed north. "It's funny," Robinson said with a touch of sadness, "you think you're doing things right and it all goes wrong. One of my kids has a knack for trouble. I don't know why. He's going to be all right. I know that. But he's rebelled against everything my wife and I have stood for."

"Mr. Robinson," I ventured, "weren't you a rebel? A rebel with a cause?"

"No," he said. "I just wanted to play ball."

Home, finally. Jackie Robinson carried my suitcase to the door and wished me well. He motioned to the soldier to move up front, and both waved goodbye as the car edged out of sight.

Sitting with a cup of coffee I wondered how to explain to my kids who this hero was; how to explain the brouhaha 40 years ago over a black man playing in the major leagues. Then I thought about the courage it took for that young man to walk into that stadium and face a hostile crowd—alone. I'll tell my children about that man. ❖

❋ What is your impression of Jackie Robinson after reading this story?

_____

_____

_____

_____

❋ With a partner, select three key words that could characterize Jackie Robinson, based on the perspectives you have read in this unit. Write those words with a brief reason for each one here.

_____

_____

_____

_____

_____

_____

The perspective of a stranger can focus attention on the details of the story rather than on the person who tells it.

© GREAT SOURCE. COPYING IS PROHIBITED.

© GREAT SOURCE. COPYING IS PROHIBITED.

Focusing on Language and Craft

In this unit, you will read **personal narrative and poetry** in which writers express personal thoughts and make connections. You will hear the voices of contemporary teenagers and established poets, like Langston Hughes. As you read, you will also be writing. Sometimes you will write back to the writers themselves; sometimes you will write to people you want to hear you, to know you for who you are, inside.

The poet e. e. cummings said, "To be nobody but yourself—in a world which is doing its best, night and day, to make you like everybody else—means to fight the hardest battle which any human being can fight; and never stop fighting." All the narrators in this unit are trying to be "nobody but" themselves.

In Jacqueline Woodson's book *Locomotion,* we learn that Lonnie Collins Motion, nicknamed "Locomotion," lost both his parents when he was seven years old. Now eleven, he's learning how to put his feelings on paper, into poems.

Here's Locomotion's first poem. Read it once just to find out what it says.

Response Notes

Who's Miss Edna?

from **Locomotion** by Jacqueline Woodson

This whole book's a poem 'cause every time I try to
tell the whole story my mind goes *Be quiet!*
Only it's not my mind's voice,
it's Miss Edna's over and over and over
Be quiet!

I'm not a really loud kid, I swear. I'm just me and
sometimes I maybe make a little bit of noise.
If I was a grown-up maybe Miss Edna
wouldn't always be telling me to be quiet
but I'm eleven and maybe eleven's just noisy.

Maybe twelve's quieter.

But when Miss Edna's voice comes on, the ideas in my
head go out like a candle and all you see left is this little
string of smoke that disappears real quick
before I even have a chance to find out
what it's trying to say.

So this whole book's a poem because poetry's short and

this whole book's a poem 'cause Ms. Marcus says
write it down before it leaves your brain.
I tell her about the smoke and she says
Good, Lonnie, write that.
Not a whole lot of people be saying *Good, Lonnie* to me
so I write the string-of-smoke thing down real fast.
Ms. Marcus says *We'll worry about line breaks later.*

Write fast, Lonnie, Ms. Marcus says.
And I'm thinking Yeah, I better write fast before Miss
Edna's voice comes on and blows my candle idea out. ❖

© GREAT SOURCE. COPYING IS PROHIBITED.

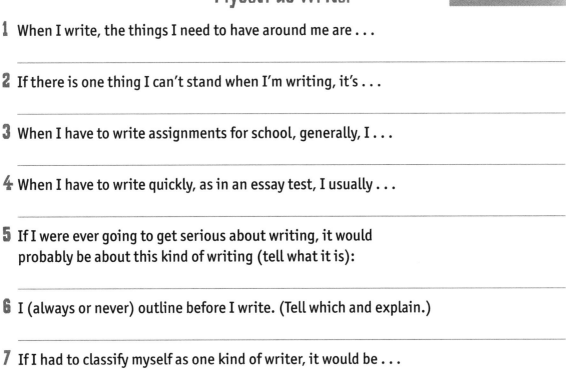

✳ Now go back and read the poem again, this time using the **Response Notes** column to write what you're thinking or wondering as you read.

✳ With a partner or group, talk about the poem. Here are some questions to get you started:
  ■ What do you know about Lonnie so far?
  ■ What do you think Lonnie means about the "string-of-smoke thing"?
  ■ Can you guess yet who Miss Edna is? If so, who is she to Lonnie?

✳ In this unit, along with reading the thoughts, ideas, and personal stories of teenagers, you're also going to write your own pieces. Before starting to write, here is a questionnaire that will help you picture yourself as a writer. Jot down your responses in the space provided.

Myself as Writer

1 When I write, the things I need to have around me are . . .

_____

2 If there is one thing I can't stand when I'm writing, it's . . .

_____

3 When I have to write assignments for school, generally, I . . .

_____

4 When I have to write quickly, as in an essay test, I usually . . .

_____

5 If I were ever going to get serious about writing, it would probably be about this kind of writing (tell what it is):

_____

6 I (always or never) outline before I write. (Tell which and explain.)

_____

7 If I had to classify myself as one kind of writer, it would be . . .

_____

✳ Look for some connections among the answers you wrote on page 71. Do one or two aspects of you as a writer emerge? Draw a picture of yourself as a writer. The drawing might be symbolic, impressionistic, or realistic.

✳ Explain your picture and tell how it represents you as a writer.

_____

_____

_____

_____

_____

_____

_____

_____

_____

_____

© GREAT SOURCE. COPYING IS PROHIBITED.

✳ At the beginning of the book *Locomotion,* Lonnie writes,

> Name all the people
> You're always thinking about
> People are poems.

In this lesson, you will write a poem about the people "you're always thinking about." They can be family, friends, teachers, celebrities, sports figures, whoever captures your attention.

To plan your writing:

■ Begin by just clustering their names in a web.

■ In the same oval, write a word or phrase that describes that person.

■ Then write the name of something you associate with that individual on a spoke.

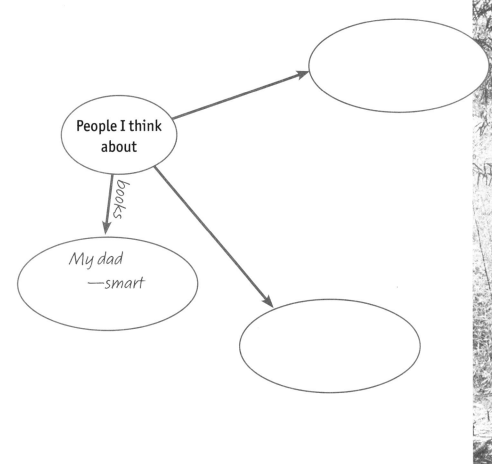

© GREAT SOURCE. COPYING IS PROHIBITED.

✳ Using some of the names and words from your list or cluster, write a poem about the people you think about often. You might title it "People Are Poems" or another title you choose.

✳ Share your poem with your partner or group. Notice how different people chose to write their poems. Remember to frame your comments in positive ways. Talk about the decisions you each made about what to write. Did you all break your poems up into lines? Here's what Lonnie says about that:

> Ms. Marcus
> says
> line breaks help
> us figure out
> what matters
> to the poet
> *Don't jumble your ideas*
> Ms. Marcus says
> *Every line*
> *should count.*

Writers can use poetry to express their thoughts and feelings.

Ask yourself: does every line in my poem count? If not, you can always change it. That's the beauty of writing. You can always make changes when you think of a way to make it say more clearly what you mean.

Ms. Marcus, Lonnie C. Motion's teacher, taught the class about a different kind of poem. It's called an **epistle poem,** which means a letter written as a poem. Here's how Lonnie describes it in a letter to his father. (His father and mother had both died in a fire.)

from **Locomotion** by Jacqueline Woodson

Hey Pops,
   Today our teacher showed us this poem by this poet guy named Langston Hughes. It made me remember something. That long time ago when you read us that goodnight poem about that guy who loved his friend...

Lonnie goes on to explain to his father that an epistle poem is written as a letter. In his letter, he says,

   I didn't know a letter could be a kind of poem. So now I'm writing one to you to say that even though we can't do stuff like go to the park on our bikes...even though we can't do that kind of stuff no more, I haven't forgot none of it. I'm gonna go see if I can find that poem about the guy loving his friend. I hope it's by Langston Hughes.
   Love, Locomotion ✛

Response Notes

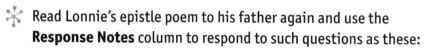

✳ Read Lonnie's epistle poem to his father again and use the **Response Notes** column to respond to such questions as these:
   ■ Where is it suggested that Lonnie's father is dead?
   ■ Are there any places in the poem where Lonnie's use of non-standard English or spelling makes it hard to understand? If so, mark them.

✳ Talk with your group about Lonnie's epistle poem. Use these suggestions to get started.
   ■ Talk about your Response Notes.
   ■ Talk about whether you think Lonnie's epistle poem is a poem.
      What makes it seem like a poem?
      What makes it seem like ordinary prose?
   ■ Talk about whether you ever "talk" to someone who isn't right there with you.

© GREAT SOURCE. COPYING IS PROHIBITED.

WRITING YOUR OWN EPISTLE POEM

✳ Write an epistle poem. You might write to a grandparent, your mother, your father, a friend, or a coach. When you write your epistle poem, keep these tips in mind:

- Write it in the form of a letter.
- Make clear to whom you're writing and whether the person is alive or not.
- Write as Lonnie did, from the heart.
- Use the language that you use in everyday speech—comfortable, informal language like Lonnie used in his poems.

_____

_____

_____

_____

_____

_____

_____

✳ Share your poem with a partner or your group. See how it feels to read your poem aloud. Does it sound as if it is in your own voice? Does it sound like you are speaking, or does it sound artificial or false?

REVISING

✳ As you read your work aloud, you might find that there are words or phrases that you'd like to change. **Revising** your work is part of the act of writing. Look carefully at your epistle poem and make any changes you think would make it a stronger letter poem. Use these suggestions for revising:

- Look for places where you could be more specific.
- Add sensory language when it is appropriate.
- Mention your relationship with the person you are writing to.
- Be sure you are writing honestly; remember that Ms. Marcus told her class "every line should count."

An epistle poem helps you focus on your audience because it is written to a specific person.

✳ When you have made the changes you want to make, copy your poem and sign it.

© GREAT SOURCE. COPYING IS PROHIBITED.

In *Bronx Masquerade* by Nikki Grimes, Wesley "Bad Boy" Boone explains that his teacher, Mr. Ward, had the class reading poetry from the Harlem Renaissance for about a month. "Then Mr. Ward asked us to write an essay about it. Make sense to you? Me neither. I mean, what's the point of studying *poetry* and then writing *essays?* So I wrote a bunch of poems instead."

That was the beginning of the poetry revolution. Wesley not only wrote "a bunch of poems," he wanted to read them to the class. The first poem he wrote was about one of the most important of the Harlem Renaissance poets, **Langston Hughes.** Remember that Lonnie mentioned "this poet guy" Hughes in his epistle poem to his father.

Before you read Wesley's poem in Lesson 24, however, read a poem by Langston Hughes. That way you will share with Wesley and the other students what they had been reading in class. Note images of what life has been like for the mother in your **Response Notes.**

Mother to Son by Langston Hughes

Well, son, I'll tell you:
Life for me ain't been no crystal stair.
It's had tacks in it,
And splinters,
And boards torn up,
And places with no carpet on the floor—
Bare.
But all the time
I'se been a-climbin' on,
And reachin' landin's,
And turnin' corners,
And sometimes goin' in the dark
Where there ain't been no light.
So, boy, don't you turn back.
Don't you set down on the steps.
'Cause you finds it's kinder hard.
Don't you fall now—
For I'se still goin', honey,
I'se still climbin',
And life for me ain't been no crystal stair. ❖

© GREAT SOURCE. COPYING IS PROHIBITED.

DRAWING THE POEM

✳ Using the images in the poem as guidelines, draw what life has been like for the mother in this poem. Under your drawing, write a sentence that you think describes the mother.

_____

_____

_____

_____

_____

© GREAT SOURCE. COPYING IS PROHIBITED.

DISCUSSION

■ What do you think Hughes means by the terms *splinter* and *crystal stair?*

■ In your group, talk about how life has been for the mother in the poem. Use the images of *splinters* and *crystal stair* in your discussion.

■ What do you think is the most important thing the mother tells the son?

✳ Write a paragraph in which you talk about some of the *splinters* or *crystal stairs* in your own life or in the lives of your parents.

Poetic metaphors can convey powerful thoughts in everyday language.

© GREAT SOURCE. COPYING IS PROHIBITED.

Every Friday, Mr. Ward, the teacher in *Bronx Masquerade,* holds an Open Mike session for his students to read their poems. Here's the poem Wesley "Bad Boy" Boone read after the class studied Langston Hughes's poems. In your **Response Notes,** list wording and images you find interesting. Tell why.

Response Notes

Long Live Langston from *Bronx Masquerade*
by Nikki Grimes

Trumpeter of Lenox and 7th
Through Jesse B. Semple,
you simply celebrated
Blues and Be-bop
and being Black before
it was considered hip.
You dipped into
the muddy waters
of the Harlem River
and shouted "taste and see"
that we Black folk be good
at fanning hope
and stoking the fires
of dreams deferred.
You made sure
the world heard
about the beauty of
maple sugar children, and the
artfully tattooed backs of Black
sailors venturing out
to foreign places.
Your Sweet Flypaper of Life
led us past the Apollo and on
through 125th and all the other
Harlem streets you knew like
the black of your hand.
You were a pied-piper, brother man
with poetry as your flute.
It's my honor and pleasure to salute
you, a true Renaissance man
of Harlem. ❖

© GREAT SOURCE. COPYING IS PROHIBITED.

❈ Notice how Wesley Boone got **ideas** from reading. Make a list
of things you think could trigger a poem for you. Include things
you've read, things you've seen, or encounters with other people.

_____

_____

_____

_____

_____

_____

_____

_____

_____

_____

Save this list for the next lesson.

Poets find inspiration for their poems
from the world around them—from their
friends and family, from their reading,
from the experiences they have had.

LESSON 25

CONNECTING THROUGH POETRY

Two of the students in Mr. Ward's class, Leslie and Porscha, discovered when they ran into each other in the locker room that they had both lost their mothers. Although they had not liked each other before, they unexpectedly became friends. Their **connection** led them to sharing their poetry in Mr. Ward's class and changed not only how they felt about school, but how they felt about themselves.

Read this section of Porscha's journal, written toward the end of the school year.

Response Notes

"Porscha's Journal" from *Bronx Masquerade*
by Nikki Grimes

Leslie says I've got to learn to let people in, and I know she's right. Poetry just may be a way to do that. I mean, it worked for Devon, didn't it? And Tyrone. We all got to see another side of them. Even Janelle gets up there—Miss Shyness herself! I've never seen her turn so bold, although the boldness only seems to last as long as she's up front reading her poems. Still, that's something. Tyrone was the biggest surprise, though. Who would have guessed he wrote poetry? And he knows his poems by heart, no less.

The first time he got up there, I rolled my eyes like half the sisters in class, certain he was going to spout something lame.... But there was nothing lame about this poem.... It was about what's going on in the world, and about trying to make sense of it. It was a poem by somebody who really thinks about things, and that somebody turned out to be Tyrone. He made me change my mind about him that day. Maybe I can change people's minds about me too. It's worth a shot. I better do it quick, though. There are only a few Open Mike Fridays left before school's out, and the last one will be at assembly, and I don't plan on getting up in front of a whole group of strangers my first time out.

Friday is two days away, and I know exactly what poem I'm going to read. ❖

In Leslie's journal, she recounted her conversation with Porscha. Porscha told Leslie how she was ashamed of her mother and how she died. She had never said good-bye to her mother or forgiven her for dying. The poem that Porscha read to her class during that Friday's Open Mike session ended with the line, "Mom, I finally forgive you. Good-bye, Love, Porscha."

© GREAT SOURCE. COPYING IS PROHIBITED.

What you discover when you read the poems from the sophomores in Mr. Ward's class is that writing and sharing their poetry created a class bond that was powerful. For the first time they saw each other honestly, through the masquerade that had kept them apart before. They saw each other change, growing in understanding of themselves and each other.

✳ Imagine that you are getting ready to read a poem to your class. Think about the relationships you have with your friends. Think about how you might like to get to know some of the other students whom you don't know too well.

✳ Look back at the list you made at the end of the last lesson. Feel free to add to it now. Then choose one event from your list— something you did with another person, something you read, something you viewed in a special way—and write about it as a journal entry.

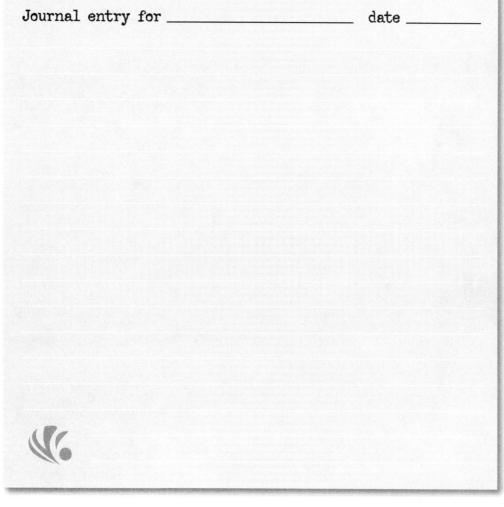

Journal entry for _____ date _____

© GREAT SOURCE. COPYING IS PROHIBITED.

The difference between a journal entry and a poem is that a poem focuses on just one idea. Try to pick out the key event or emotion and focus on that. Remember how in the first lessons in this unit Lonnie's teacher, Ms. Marcus, told them that *every line should count* in a poem.

✳ Now use some of the ideas from your journal entry to write a poem.

- In your poem use the natural language of your own speech, as the students in Mr. Drew's class did.

- Focus on one event or emotion. Use concrete images and sensory language.

- Be sure to write honestly. But if there is something you don't want to share, don't put it in this poem.

- Think about the way poets make comparisons using similes or metaphors. Don't force them, but if they come naturally, be sure to include them.

_____

_____

_____

_____

_____

_____

_____

_____

_____

_____

_____

_____

_____

_____

_____

_____

Writing and sharing poems helps create strong connections between people.

© GREAT SOURCE. COPYING IS PROHIBITED.

© GREAT SOURCE. COPYING IS PROHIBITED.

Studying an Author

For a good part of her childhood, **Yoshiko Uchida** felt very much alone. She was born in Alameda, California, the daughter of two Japanese immigrants. Because her parents were Japanese and she was American, she sometimes felt as if she didn't belong. To avoid getting bored, young Yoshiko turned to writing. She started out writing stories about Japanese and Japanese American children. When she was in her early twenties, she published many of her articles and folk tales about Japan. Later, she switched her focus and began writing about Japanese Americans and their experiences before, during, and after World War II.

In this unit you'll explore the works of Yoshiko Uchida. As you read, watch for questions, experiences, and feelings that remind you of yourself. How is your search for an identity similar to that of Uchida?

Yoshiko Uchida often writes about people who are searching for an **identity.** "Who am I?" "Where do I belong?" "How do I fit in?" These are questions that many of Uchida's characters ask themselves over and over again. They are also questions that Uchida as a young girl asked herself.

For Yoshiko Uchida, the search for an identity began some two thousand miles from home. Determined to find her identity, Uchida traveled to Japan. While there, she spent most of her time learning everything she could about Japan—its customs, its history, and its people. During this period she found part of the answer to the question, "Who am I?"

Read this excerpt from the folk tale "The Princess of Light." As you read, underline words and phrases that show Uchida's respect for Japanese customs and history. In your **Response Notes,** mention any personal connections you can make to this story.

Response Notes

from "**The Princess of Light**" by Yoshiko Uchida

Once upon a time, there was an old man and an old woman who lived in a small village in Japan. Their little wooden house with the low thatched roof stood nestled against a hillside covered with trees. Each day the old man strapped his straw sandals on his feet and went out to the nearby bamboo thicket to cut down long, slender stalks of bamboo. When he brought them home, the old woman would help him cut and polish the smooth stalks. Then together they would make bamboo vases, baskets, flutes, and many beautiful ornaments which they could sell in the village.

This reminds me of another folk tale I've read.

They were good, kind, and honest people, and they worked very hard. They were happy, but they were lonesome, for they had no children. Both of them wanted a child more than anything else in the world.

"Oh, if only we had a little boy or a little girl, how happy we would be," sighed the old man.

"Yes, wouldn't that be wonderful!" answered the old woman. "I would rather have a child than all the riches on earth!"

And so each day they both knelt at the little shrine in the corner of their room, and prayed that some day they would be granted a child.

Now one day when the old man went out into the bamboo thicket, he saw one stalk which was shining so brightly it looked as though it were made of gold. He hurried toward it and looked at it closely, but he could not tell what made it shine.

© GREAT SOURCE. COPYING IS PROHIBITED.

"My, what a strange bamboo," said the old man to himself. "Perhaps I'd better see what is inside." So he began to cut it down with the saw which he carried at his side. But suddenly he stopped, for he heard something very strange!

"What was that?" asked the old man. "It sounded like the crying of a baby!"

He straightened his back and looked all around, but he did not see anyone. All he could see were the stalks of bamboo swaying gently in the breeze.

He shook his head slowly and said, "My, I must be getting old to be hearing such strange sounds in a bamboo thicket."

He was turning again toward the shining bamboo when he heard the sound once more. He was sure this time that it was a baby crying, and the sound came right from inside the strange shiny stalk. Quickly he cut down the bamboo and looked inside the hollow of the stalk. There he saw a tiny baby girl! She looked up at the old man and smiled sweetly. And the old man was so surprised at this strange sight, he blinked hard and touched the little girl to see if she were real.

"My goodness! Good gracious! Oya-oya!" was all the old man could say. "This child must have been sent to us straight from heaven," he thought, as he picked her up very carefully. Then he quickly started homeward, for he could scarcely wait to show her to the old woman.

When the old woman saw the beautiful child, she threw up her hands in surprise. "God has been good to us!" she exclaimed. "We must take very good care of our little girl." Then she hurriedly set about spreading a quilt on the floor where she gently laid the new baby.

The next morning the old man was up bright and early. He whistled gaily as he walked toward the bamboo thicket. As he came closer to the spot where he had found the little baby the day before, he saw another bamboo which was shining brightly.

"I wonder if I will find another little baby," thought the old man, as he prepared to cut down the bamboo. He listened for any sound that might be the crying of a child, but he heard only the song of a sparrow as it flew into the thicket. This time, when he cut down the shiny bamboo stalk, a shower of gold coins fell to the ground. They glittered and sparkled, and seemed to tell

© GREAT SOURCE. COPYING IS PROHIBITED.

the old man, "Take us home. We are yours!" The old man gathered up the coins and filled his moneybag. Then he hurried home once more, chuckling softly to himself to think how he would again surprise his wife.

When the old woman saw the coins, she said, "My, how lucky we are! Perhaps this is God's way of helping us provide for our little daughter. We must be grateful and take good care of her."

"Yes, yes, we shall always work hard and take good care of our child," said the old man.

From that day on, each time the old man went out to the bamboo thicket, he found one shiny golden stalk. When he cut it down, he always found the hollow filled with gold coins. Before long, the old man and woman became rich, but they continued to work hard.

The little baby of the bamboo was a wonderful child indeed. Each night she seemed to grow a whole year older, instead of just a day older. Each morning she surprised the old man and woman by being able to do or say something new.

"My, but she is a bright child," said the old woman.

"And see how much more beautiful she becomes each day," added the old man.

As she grew older, they discovered something even more wonderful about her. A beautiful, bright light seemed to glow all around her, just like the light which the old man had seen around the bamboo in which he found her. So the old man and woman decided to call their lovely daughter Kaguya Hime, which means Princess of Light. Their little home seemed to be filled with golden sunlight day and night, and they no longer had to use the lamps in the evening.

Kaguya Hime continued to grow in beauty each day, until soon the whole countryside had heard of her loveliness and of the radiant glow which she cast about her.

"She is like a lovely golden sunbeam," said some. "She is like sunshine on a rainbow," said others. "She is an angel from heaven," said still others; and everyone who knew her came to love her dearly. ❖

✳ Based on what you've read, what would you say is Uchida's attitude toward Japan?

_____

_____

_____

_____

_____

© GREAT SOURCE. COPYING IS PROHIBITED.

✳ What connection can you make between "The Princess of Light" and the questions "Who am I?" and "Where do I belong?"

_____

_____

_____

_____

_____

_____

✳ Imagine you are twenty-year-old Yoshiko Uchida on an extended stay in Japan. Write a letter home to your parents. In your letter, explain your answers to the questions "Who am I?" and "Where do I belong?"

_____

_____

_____

_____

_____

_____

_____

_____

_____

_____

_____

_____

_____

_____

Authors, like many people, explore questions such as "Who am I?" and "Where do I belong?"

© GREAT SOURCE. COPYING IS PROHIBITED.

Because she was an American, Uchida wrote about Japan from an American perspective. For example, in *The Forever Christmas Tree,* Uchida tells the story of a Japanese boy who longs for a Christmas tree, even though his family does not celebrate Christmas:

> It was too cold to play outside, so Takashi sat where he could watch the road. He waited and waited for Kaya to come home from school. When at last he saw her, she was running, and Takashi knew she had something special to tell. As soon as she was in the house, the words came tumbling out.
>
> "Today we learned about Christmas!" she said, and the bright glow of her excitement quickly spilled out to fill Takashi too.
>
> Takashi did not know much about Christmas for no one celebrated it in Sugi Village. It was the New Year that mattered.

At times, Uchida felt torn between these two different cultures. In her **autobiography,** she describes how, as a child, she often felt as if she were being pulled in two completely different directions, never quite knowing who she was, or how she fit in. As you read this excerpt from Uchida's autobiography, underline or highlight information about the author's sense of identity. Note the connections to your life in the **Response Notes** column.

from **The Invisible Thread** by Yoshiko Uchida

Response Notes

I was born in California, recited the Pledge of Allegiance to the flag each morning at school, and loved my country as much as any other American— maybe even more.

Still, there was a large part of me that was Japanese simply because Mama and Papa had passed on to me so much of their own Japanese spirit and soul. Their own values of loyalty, honor, self-discipline, love, and respect for one's parents, teachers, and superiors were all very much a part of me.

I hate when teachers mispronounce my name!

There was also my name, which teachers couldn't seem to pronounce properly even when I shortened my first name to Yoshi. And there was my Japanese face, which closed more and more doors to me as I grew older.

How wonderful it would be, I used to think, if I had blond hair and blue eyes like Marian and Solveig. Or a name like Mary Anne Brown or Betty Johnson.

If only I didn't have to ask such questions as, "Can we come swim in your pool? We're Japanese." Or when we were looking for a house, "Will the neighbors object if we move in next door?" Or when I went for my first professional haircut, "Do you cut Japanese hair?"

© GREAT SOURCE. COPYING IS PROHIBITED.

Still, I didn't truly realize how different I was until the summer I was eleven. Although Papa usually went on business trips alone, bringing back such gifts as silver pins for Mama or charm bracelets for Keiko and me, that summer he was able to take us along, thanks to a railroad pass.

We took the train, stopping at the Grand Canyon, Houston, New Orleans, Washington, D.C., New York, Boston, Niagara Falls, and on the way home, Chicago, to see the World's Fair.

Crossing the Mississippi River was a major event, as our train rolled onto a barge and sailed slowly over that grand body of water. We all got off the train for a closer look, and I was so impressed with the river's majesty, I felt impelled to make some kind of connection with it. Finally, I leaned over the barge rail and spit so a part of me would be in the river forever.

For my mother, the high point of the trip was a visit to the small village of Cornwall, Connecticut. There she had her first meeting with the two white American pen pals with whom she had corresponded since her days at Doshisha University. She also visited one of her former missionary teachers, Louise DeForest, who had retired there. And it was there I met a young girl my age, named Cathy Sellew. We became good friends, corresponded for many years, and met again as adults when I needed a home and a friend.

Everyone in the village greeted us warmly, and my father was asked to say a few words to the children of the Summer Vacation Church School—which he did with great relish.

Most of the villagers had never before met a Japanese American. One smiling woman shook my hand and said, "My, but you speak English so beautifully." She had meant to compliment me, but I was so astonished, I didn't know what to say. I realized she had seen only my outer self—my Japanese face—and addressed me as a foreigner. I knew then that I would always be different, even though I wanted so badly to be like my white American friends. ❖

✳ What are three things you learned about Uchida from reading this excerpt?

1. _____

    _____

2. _____

    _____

3. _____

    _____

© GREAT SOURCE. COPYING IS PROHIBITED.

✳ As a child, Uchida felt as if she were three children rolled into one. Sometimes she was Japanese, sometimes she was American, and sometimes she was Japanese American. Review the notes you made while reading the excerpt from *The Invisible Thread*. Complete the chart below by listing some of the ways Uchida felt as if she were three little girls in one.

YOSHIKO UCHIDA AS A CHILD

I am Japanese	I am Japanese American	I am American
My name is Japanese		

When you read an autobiography, watch for the ways the author answers the questions "Who am I?" and "How do I fit in?" These questions will help you see how the author views himself or herself.

© GREAT SOURCE. COPYING IS PROHIBITED.

During World War II, more than 120,000 West Coast Japanese Americans were uprooted from their homes and sent to U.S. government detention camps in the desert. Men, women, and children were imprisoned for as long as three years, for no other reason than that they were of Japanese ancestry. The majority of those imprisoned were U.S. citizens.

In 1942, Yoshiko Uchida and her family were "relocated" to a horse stall at Tanforan racetrack in San Bruno, California. Later they were moved to Topaz, a Japanese American internment camp in Utah. The Uchida family spent many long, frightening months at Topaz.

For years after she was released, Yoshiko kept quiet about the alienation and rejection she felt as a result of her internment. In the early 1970s, however, she decided she would remain silent no longer. She wrote a series of books—fiction and nonfiction—that describe the experiences of her family and friends.

In her books about the detention camps, Uchida uses **sensory language** (words that can help you see, hear, touch, smell, or taste the thing described) as a way of giving readers a "you are there" feeling. As you read this excerpt from *Journey Home,* underline words and phrases that help you see, hear, feel, smell, and even taste what it was like at the detention center in Topaz. Record your reactions to her experiences in your **Response Notes.**

Response Notes

from **Journey Home** by Yoshiko Uchida

I can't see, Yuki thought frantically. I can't breathe.

The screaming desert wind flung its white powdery sand in her face, stifling her and wrapping her up in a smothering cocoon of sand so fine it was like dust. It blinded her and choked her and made her gag as she opened her mouth to cry out.

The black tar-papered barracks on either side of the road had vanished behind the swirling dust, and Yuki was all alone in an eerie, unreal world where nothing existed except the shrieking wind and the great choking clouds of dust. Yuki stumbled on, doubled over, pushing hard against the wind, gasping as she felt the sting of sand and pebbles against her legs.

Suppose she never got back to her barrack? Suppose the wind simply picked her up and flung her out beyond the barbed wire fence into the desert? Suppose no one ever found her dried, wind-blown body out there in the sagebrush?

A cry of terror swelled up inside her. "Mama! Papa! Help me!" ❖

© GREAT SOURCE. COPYING IS PROHIBITED.

✳ What is your reaction to the passage you just read?
Explain your feelings.

_____
_____
_____
_____
_____
_____
_____
_____
_____
_____
_____
_____
_____
_____
_____
_____
_____
_____
_____
_____
_____
_____
_____
_____

© GREAT SOURCE. COPYING IS PROHIBITED.

✳ Analyze the excerpt from *Journey Home.* Put any sensory words you find into the correct space on the web. Words that help you see something go in the "Sight Words" circle; words that help you know what something feels like go in the "Touch Words" circle, and so on.

Sound Words

Sight Words

Smell Words

Sensory Language in
Journey Home

Touch Words

Taste Words

Writers use sensory language in order to give readers a "you are there" feeling.

© GREAT SOURCE. COPYING IS PROHIBITED.

Readers who are familiar with Uchida's work know that she explores two **themes** over and over again in her writing. The first theme—pride in one's ancestry—is a reflection of Uchida's own feelings about herself and her family. Her second major theme—courage during times of trouble—is especially apparent in her books about Japanese American internment camps.

As you read this excerpt from Uchida's memoir *Desert Exile,* watch for ideas that relate to these two themes. Does Uchida give the two themes equal weight in this selection? Write notes in the **Response Notes** column. (*Issei* is a term for people born in Japan who live in America; *Nisei* are the American-born children of Issei parents.)

from **Desert Exile** by Yoshiko Uchida

On my last day at school, the children of my class presented me with a clay bowl one of them had made, and they stood together, giggling and embarrassed, to sing one last song for me.

On our last Sunday, my sister and I went to say goodbye to all our friends, especially the older Issei who we knew would probably remain in camp until the end of the war.

It was hard for us to go, leaving behind our Issei parents in the desolation of that desert camp. And I imagine other Nisei felt as we did as they ventured forth into the outside world.

Because we Nisei were still relatively young at the time, it was largely the Issei who had led the way, guiding us through the devastation and trauma of our forced removal. When they were uprooted from their homes, many had just reached a point of financial security in their lives. During the war, however, they all suffered enormous losses, both tangible and intangible. The evacuation was the ultimate of the incalculable hardships and indignities they had borne over the years.

© GREAT SOURCE. COPYING IS PROHIBITED.

And yet most of our parents had continued to be steadfast and strong in spirit. Our mothers had made homes of the bleak barrack rooms, just as my own mother, in her gentle, nurturing way, had been a loving focal point for our family and friends.

Deprived of so much themselves, the Issei wanted the best for their Nisei children. Many had sacrificed to send their children to college, and they encouraged them now to leave camp to continue their education.

As my sister and I prepared for our departure, thoughts of gratitude toward our Issei parents still lay unspoken deep within us, and it was only in later years that we came to realize how much they had done for us; how much they had given us to enrich and strengthen our lives. ❖

✳ Look over the notes you made about ancestry and courage while reading the selection. In the diagram below, list the ways that Uchida explores these themes in *Desert Exile*.

Taking Pride in One's Ancestry

She is respectful of the sacrifices of the Issei.

Showing Courage in Times of Trouble

She bravely leaves her parents behind.

© GREAT SOURCE. COPYING IS PROHIBITED.

✳ Now connect one of Uchida's themes to your own life. Write a journal entry describing a time you showed courage or a time you demonstrated pride in your heritage.

Journal entry for _____ date _____

_____

_____

_____

_____

_____

_____

_____

_____

_____

_____

_____

_____

_____

_____

_____

_____

Understanding an author's themes can help you connect your reading to your own life.

© GREAT SOURCE. COPYING IS PROHIBITED.

Some authors write to entertain their readers. Others write in order to argue or persuade. Still others write so that they can teach readers about something that is important or meaningful. Many writers try to do a little bit of each.

What is Uchida's **purpose,** or intent? Read this excerpt from an interview with Yoshiko Uchida. Underline any clues about her purpose. Be sure to note your questions in the **Response Notes.**

from an **interview** with Yoshiko Uchida

Response Notes

I hope to give young Asians a sense of their own history. At the same time, I want to dispel the stereotypic image still held by many non-Asians about the Japanese Americans and write about them as real people. I hope to convey as well the strength of spirit and the sense of hope and purpose I have seen in many of the first generation Japanese Americans. Beyond that, I write to celebrate our common humanity, for I feel the basic elements of humanity are present in all our strivings. ❖

✳ Summarize in your own words Uchida's purpose for writing.

_____

_____

_____

✳ Think about this passage and other writings by Yoshiko Uchida. What have you learned from reading Uchida's works?

_____

_____

_____

_____

_____

_____

_____

© GREAT SOURCE. COPYING IS PROHIBITED.

Reflect on what you know about Yoshiko Uchida—her life and her works. Use the graphic organizer below to make notes about her stories, themes, and messages.

YOSHIKO UCHIDA: WRITER, STORYTELLER, TEACHER

What she writes about	In what selection?	What lesson does she want to teach?

Some authors write with the intention of conveying to you, the reader, something they believe is important or meaningful.

© GREAT SOURCE. COPYING IS PROHIBITED.

© GREAT SOURCE. COPYING IS PROHIBITED.

Assessing Your Growing Repertoire

At this point in the *Daybook,* you have been introduced to a number of ways to become a better reader and a better writer. You have learned different strategies for interacting and connecting with the stories or essays you have read. You have experimented with multiple perspectives. You have examined language and craft. You have focused on one particular author.

Now you are going to combine those skills and strategies in one unit. In this unit, you will read a short story by Jane Yolen, and then participate in a number of reading and writing activities designed to show how well you organize and express your ideas. You will demonstrate how you use the skills and strategies presented in the *Daybook*. You will work both individually and in groups as you read, talk, draw, and write.

After you have written and revised your essay, you will evaluate your own work. You will consider what you need to do to improve your skills as you continue to strengthen your use of **critical reading and writing strategies.**

Ten children's authors were asked to write a story based on the idea that one beautifully wrapped birthday gift is empty. Here is Jane Yolen's response to that challenge. As you read "Birthday Box" by Jane Yolen, use the **Response Notes** column. Remember you can draw or write, make predictions, ask questions, comment on what surprises you, and **make connections** to what you already know or have experienced. Show how well you have learned the strategies in the previous lessons by making your annotations as complete as you can.

© GREAT SOURCE. COPYING IS PROHIBITED.

"Birthday Box" by Jane Yolen

Response Notes

I was ten years old when my mother died. Ten years old on that very day. Still she gave me a party of sorts. Sick as she was, Mama had seen to it, organizing it at the hospital. She made sure the doctors and nurses all brought me presents. We were good friends with them all by that time, because Mama had been in the hospital for so long.

The head nurse, V. Louise Higgins (I never did know what that V stood for), gave me a little box, which was sort of funny because she was the biggest of all the nurses there. I mean she was tremendous. And she was the only one who insisted on wearing all white. Mama had called her the great white shark when she was first admitted, only not to V. Louise's face. "All those needles," Mama had said. "Like teeth." But V. Louise was sweet, not sharklike at all, and she'd been so gentle with Mama.

I opened the little present first. It was a fountain pen, a real one, not a fake one like you get at Kmart.

"Now you can write beautiful stories, Katie," V. Louise said to me.

I didn't say that stories come out of your head, not out of a pen. That wouldn't have been polite, and Mama—even sick— was real big on politeness.

"Thanks, V. Louise," I said.

The Stardust Twins—which is what Mama called Patty and Tracey-lynn because they reminded her of dancers in an oldfashioned ballroom—gave me a present together. It was a diary and had a picture of a little girl in pink, reading in a garden swing. A little young for me, a little too cute. I mean, I read Stephen King and want to write like him. But as Mama always reminded me whenever Dad finally remembered to send me something, it was the thought that counted, not the actual gift.

"It's great," I told them. "I'll write in it with my new pen." And I wrote my name on the first page just to show them I meant it.

They hugged me and winked at Mama. She tried to wink back but was just too tired and shut both her eyes instead.

Lily, who is from Jamaica, had baked me some sweet bread. Mary Margaret gave me a gold cross blessed by the pope, which I put on even though Mama and I weren't churchgoers. That was Dad's thing.

Then Dr. Dann, the intern who was on days, and Dr. Pucci, the oncologist (which is the fancy name for a cancer doctor), gave me a big box filled to the top with little presents, each wrapped up individually. All things they knew I'd love— paperback books and writing paper and erasers with funny animal heads and colored paper clips and a rubber stamp that printed FROM KATIE'S DESK and other stuff. They must have raided a stationery store.

There was one box, though, they held out till the end. It was about the size of a large top hat. The paper was deep blue and covered with stars; not fake stars but real stars, I mean, like a map of the night sky. The ribbon was two shades of blue with silver threads running through. There was no name on the card.

"Who's it from?" I asked.

None of the nurses answered, and the doctors both suddenly were studying the ceiling tiles with the kind of intensity they usually saved for X rays. No one spoke. In fact the only sound for the longest time was Mama's breathing machine going in and out and in and out. It was a harsh, horrible, insistent sound, and usually I talked and talked to cover up the noise. But I was waiting for someone to tell me.

At last V. Louise said, "It's from your mama, Katie. She told us what she wanted. And where to get it."

I turned and looked at Mama then, and her eyes were open again. Funny, but sickness had made her even more beautiful than good health had. Her skin was like that old paper, the kind they used to write on with quill pens, and stretched out over her bones so she looked like a model. Her eyes, which had been a deep, brilliant blue, were now like the fall sky, bleached and softened. She was like a faded photograph of herself. She smiled a very small smile at me. I knew it was an effort.

"It's you," she mouthed. I read her lips. I had gotten real good at that. I thought she meant it was a present for me.

"Of course it is," I said cheerfully. I had gotten good at that, too, being cheerful when I didn't feel like it. "Of course it is."

I took the paper off the box carefully, not tearing it but folding it into a tidy packet. I twisted the ribbons around my hand and then put them on the pillow by her hand. It made the stark white hospital bed look almost festive.

Under the wrapping, the box was beautiful itself. It was made of a heavy cardboard and covered with a linen material that had a pattern of cloud-filled skies.

I opened the box slowly and . . .

© GREAT SOURCE. COPYING IS PROHIBITED.

"It's empty," I said. "Is this a joke?" I turned to ask Mama, but she was gone. I mean, her body was there, but she wasn't. It was as if she was as empty as the box.

Dr. Pucci leaned over her and listened with a stethoscope, then almost absently patted Mama's head. Then, with infinite care, V. Louise closed Mama's eyes, ran her hand across Mama's cheek, and turned off the breathing machine.

"Mama!" I cried. And to the nurses and doctors, I screamed, "Do something!" And because the room had suddenly become so silent, my voice echoed back at me. "Mama, do something."

I cried steadily for, I think, a week. Then I cried at night for a couple of months. And then for about a year I cried at anniversaries, like Mama's birthday or mine, at Thanksgiving, on Mother's Day. I stopped writing. I stopped reading except for school assignments. I was pretty mean to my half brothers and totally rotten to my stepmother and Dad. I felt empty and angry, and they all left me pretty much alone.

And then one night, right after my first birthday without Mama, I woke up remembering how she had said, "It's you." Not, "It's for you," just "It's you." Now Mama had been a high school English teacher and a writer herself. She'd had poems published in little magazines. She didn't use words carelessly. In the end she could hardly use any words at all. So—I asked myself in that dark room—why had she said, "It's you"? Why were they the very last words she had ever said to me, forced out with her last breath?

I turned on the bedside light and got out of bed. The room was full of shadows, not all of them real.

Pulling the desk chair over to my closet, I climbed up and felt along the top shelf, and against the back wall, there was the birthday box, just where I had thrown it the day I had moved in with my dad.

I pulled it down and opened it. It was as empty as the day I had put it away.

"It's you," I whispered to the box.

And then suddenly I knew.

Mama had meant *I* was the box, solid and sturdy, maybe even beautiful or at least interesting on the outside. But I had to fill up the box to make it all it could be. And I had to fill me up as well. She had guessed what might happen to me, had told me in a subtle way. In the two words she could manage.

I stopped crying and got some paper out of the desk drawer. I got out my fountain pen. I started writing, and I haven't stopped since. The first thing I wrote was about that birthday. I put it in the box, and pretty soon that box was overflowing with stories. And poems. And memories.

And so was I.

And so was I. ❖

© GREAT SOURCE. COPYING IS PROHIBITED.

✳ Work with a small group to share some of your questions and ideas about the story. As you talk, use your **Response Notes** to read lines from the story that support your ideas. You can also add notes as you discuss the story.

- ■ What do the presents Katie receives on her birthday tell you about her?
- ■ What do you think about the "birthday box" at first?
- ■ How would you describe the relationship between Katie and her mother?
- ■ What do you think of the way Katie acted after her mother died?
- ■ What do you know about Katie's dad?
- ■ What did Katie's mother mean when she said, "It's you"?

MAKING CONNECTIONS

When you make connections, you are reaching beyond the story itself. Think of stories in your own life or from books, movies, or television shows that relate in some way to "Birthday Box." Your connection might be in experiencing the death of someone close to you, in remembering a memorable birthday celebration, or in finally understanding why you acted as you did at a particular time.

✳ Have you ever received a gift you did not appreciate or understand until later? What personal connection did you make to this story? Write your ideas about it here.

_____

_____

_____

_____

_____

_____

_____

_____

When you interact and connect with a story, you get more meaning out of it.

© GREAT SOURCE. COPYING IS PROHIBITED.

You know from reading and discussing "Birthday Box" that Katie loves to write. By the time she is your age, she will probably have filled her box many times with poems and stories and, as she says, memories. Perhaps she has included in her box poems and stories by other people. Can you think of a poem or story she might like well enough to put into her special box?

❋ Think about the kinds of pieces Katie might put into her box and tell why you think she would like them. You have your own ideas of Katie—her personality, her probable likes and dislikes, her actions (how she acted after her mother's death, for instance). You have your own different views, your own perspective. (Note: you can include pieces you have read in the *Daybook* as well as from other books.)

Pieces Katie might put into her box	Reasons she might save these pieces

❋ What items other than stories and poems might Katie put into her birthday box? What about CDs, movie posters, and her other favorite things? Imagine this box is much larger than it was in the story and put some of these things into it.

Suggestions for other kinds of mementos	Reasons she might include these pieces

© GREAT SOURCE. COPYING IS PROHIBITED.

Read May Swenson's poem "The Key to Everything," using the
Response Notes column as you read. Make notes about the questions
the poem raises for you.

"The Key To Everything" by May Swenson

Is there anything I can do
or has everything been done
or do
you prefer somebody else to do
it or don't
you trust me to do
it right or is it hopeless and no one
    can do a thing or do
you suppose I don't
really want to do
it and am just saying that or don't
you hear me at all or what?

You're
waiting for
the right person the doctor or
the nurse the father or
the mother or
the person with the name you keep
mumbling in your sleep
that no one ever heard of there's no one
named that really
except yourself maybe
If I knew what your name was I'd
prove it's your
own name spelled backwards or
twisted in some way the one you
keep mumbling but you
won't tell me your
name or
don't you know it
yourself that's it
of course you've
forgotten or
never quite knew it or
weren't willing to believe it

Then there *is* something I
can do I
can find your name for you
that's the key to everything
    once you'd
repeat it clearly you'd
come awake you'd
get up and walk knowing where
    you're
going where you
came from

And you'd
love me
after that or would you
hate me?
no once you'd
get there you'd
remember and love me
of course I'd
be gone by then I'd
be far away ❖

© GREAT SOURCE. COPYING IS PROHIBITED.

Sometimes you need to know the right word to help you explain a poem. The word *enigmatic* is one that could apply to May Swenson's poem "The Key to Everything." *Enigmatic* means "puzzling, or difficult to figure out." To figure out this poem, talk with a partner or group about these questions. You and your partner do not need to agree on your responses to these questions.

DISCUSSION

1 Who is the "I" of the poem? What makes you think so?

2 Who is the audience? How can you tell?

3 What might be the situation in which the speaker is saying these things?

4 Can you explain what this poem is about or what you think after reading it?

5 What is the dominant tone/mood of the poem (funny, sad, somber, questioning, etc.)?

6 How is that tone achieved?

7 How would you describe the language of the poem? What is an example?

8 How important is the title in conveying the main idea?

✳ After your discussion, choose three or more of the questions and write a paragraph explaining what you think about this poem. End your paragraph with a statement about whether you think Katie would or would not include this poem in her birthday box.

_____

_____

_____

_____

_____

_____

_____

_____

_____

> Using critical reading strategies can help you understand and remember what you read.

© GREAT SOURCE. COPYING IS PROHIBITED.

You may have read some of Jane Yolen's books, but you may not know a lot about her. Here is an interview she compiled from frequently asked questions. In the **Response Notes** column, note **connections** between Yolen's life and her writing.

Frequently Asked Questions by Jane Yolen

[Q] When did you start writing?

[A] I love writing and have always been good at it. I started as a poet and a writer of songs. I still do both. My first big success as a writer was in first grade where I wrote the class musical. It was all about vegetables and I played the chief carrot. We all ended up in a salad together! In junior high I wrote my big class essay about New York State manufacturing in verse, with a rhyme for Otis Elevators I have—thankfully—forgotten. In college I wrote my final exam in American Intellectual History in rhyme and got an A+ from a very surprised teacher.

[Q] Who were your parents?

[A] Both my parents were writers. My father was a journalist, my mother a short story writer who also created crossword puzzles and acrostics for magazines and books. So I just assumed all grownups were writers! Since my brother is a journalist, and my three grown children all write well, in our family—at any rate—that is true.

[Q] What kind of a family do you have?

[A] My husband and I have three children (Adam, Jason, Heidi); though they're all grown up now, they still give me ideas. And now that I have five granddaughters and a grandson, I am sure they will give me ideas as well!

[Q] Where do you get your ideas?

[A] I am always asked where I get my ideas from. That is a very difficult question to answer, since I get my ideas from everywhere: from things I hear and things I see, from books and songs and newspapers and paintings and conversations—and even from dreams. The storyteller in me asks: what if? And when I try to answer that, a story begins.

[Q] What awards have you won?

[A] My books have won any number of awards—the Caldecott, the Golden Kite, the Christopher Medal, the Nebula, etc. And I have won a number of body-of-work awards—the Kerlan, the Keene State, the Regina Medal. But awards just sit on the shelf gathering dust. The best awards are when young readers love my books.

© GREAT SOURCE. COPYING IS PROHIBITED.

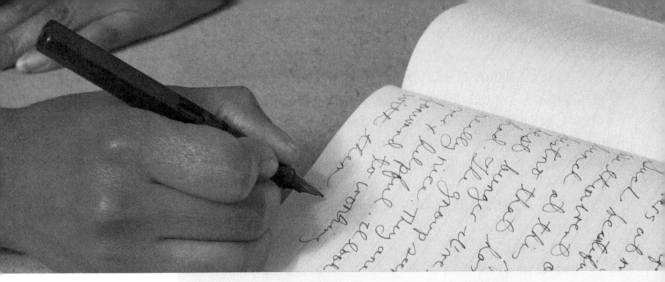

Q **What are you writing now?**

A I'm always working on something, usually several somethings. At times I am working on as many as ten projects: stories, books, poems, songs.

Q **What advice do you have for young writers?**

A I have three pieces of advice for young writers. One: read, read, read! You must read every day, and try to read a wide range of books. Two: write, write, write! Keep a journal, write letters, anything to keep the "writing muscles" in shape. Three: don't let anyone stop you from writing. Be persistent no matter what "naysayers" or critical editors have to say about your writing.

Q **Which is your favorite book you have written?**

A I don't actually have a favorite book except whatever I am working on at the moment that question is asked. That's because all the books of mine that you can read are well in my past. *Owl Moon,* for example, was published in 1987, and written at least three years earlier than that. You may have just read it, but it's a dim memory for me. So my favorite is what I am currently obsessed with, a story or poem or book which you—the reader—might not see for years yet.

Q **Who inspired your writing?**

A All the books that I have ever read inspire my own writing. My parents, both of whom were writers, were very supportive of my writing and that helped to inspire me as well.

Q **What do you do in your spare time?**

A I love to read and walk, I love traveling to foreign countries, I love to watch movies. I love to listen to music on tape and hear live music as well.

Q **What is your favorite food?**

A Chocolate cake: but alas, I can no longer eat chocolate cake. And nuts—but alas, I cannot eat them either. I can, however, eat salads of all kinds, salmon, lemon chicken, lamb chops, and carrot soup—all favorites.

© GREAT SOURCE. COPYING IS PROHIBITED.

Q **What is your favorite animal?**

A My favorite animal is the cat. My favorite cat was named Pod. Pod was a gentle, loving, golden-orange tom cat with double paws. Pod was the nicest cat we ever had. Now I share my granddaughter's cat, a lovely, feisty female black-and-white cat named Sammy.

Q **Do you ever have an idea and then lose it?**

A Every time I get an idea, I write it down and file it in my Idea File. There is no organization to it; all the ideas are jumbled together.

Q **What makes a good book?**

A Scholars and critics have been debating that question for decades. I like books that touch my head and my heart at the same time.

Q **How do you develop a style?**

A Find those narratives that you like in your favorite books. Then try to mimic those effects in your own writing. ✦

❊ Thinking of what you know about Jane Yolen now, do you have any additional insights into Katie, the main character in "Birthday Box"?

_____

_____

_____

❊ What three questions would you like to ask Jane Yolen? List them here.

_____

_____

_____

_____

> Learning about a writer's life can give you new insights into his or her writing.

© GREAT SOURCE. COPYING IS PROHIBITED.

Using what you have learned in all of the units so far, demonstrate your best reading and writing skills. Read two short prose excerpts. You will complete an exercise to help you think about the excerpts and then write an essay about them.

Think about the authors you enjoy reading. What draws you to them? Is it the subject matter they write about? Is it the form (story, poem, or novel)? Or is it the style? You know about style when it refers to the kinds of clothes you choose or the way you wear your hair. Writers have styles that depend on the choices they make in diction (word choice) and sentence structure, as well as their subject matter and point of view. You have a writing style, too, one that is changing as you develop as a writer.

When you read the following excerpts, make notes about style choices such as these:

- Does the writer use mostly short, simple sentences, more complex sentences, or a combination?
- Is the narrator directly involved in the story or on the outside?
- Is the language informal or formal?
- Are the words simple or complex?
- Does the writing include much description? Does it include action?

In the following excerpt from *The Call of the Wild* by Jack London, Buck, who is a wolf and dog hybrid, encounters a wolf.

from **The Call of the Wild** by Jack London

© GREAT SOURCE. COPYING IS PROHIBITED.

Response Notes

He had made no noise, yet it ceased from its howling and tried to sense his presence. Buck stalked into the open, half crouching, body gathered compactly together, tail straight and stiff, feet falling with unwonted care. Every movement advertised commingled threatening and overture of friendliness. It was the menacing truce that marks the meeting of wild beasts that prey. But the wolf fled at sight of him. He followed, with wild leapings, in a frenzy to overtake. He ran him into a blind channel, in the bed of the creek, where a timber jam barred the way. The wolf whirled about, pivoting on his hind legs after the fashion of Joe and of all cornered husky dogs, snarling and bristling, clipping his teeth together in a continuous and rapid succession of snaps.

Buck did not attack, but circled him about and hedged him in with friendly advances. The wolf was suspicious and afraid; for Buck made three of him in weight, while his head barely reached Buck's shoulder. Watching his chance, he darted away, and the chase was resumed. Time and again he was cornered, and the thing repeated, though he was in poor condition or Buck could not so easily have overtaken him. He would run till Buck's head was even with his flank, when he would whirl around at bay, only to dash away again at the first opportunity.

But in the end Buck's pertinacity was rewarded; for the wolf, finding that no harm was intended, finally sniffed noses with him. Then they became friendly, and played about in the nervous, half-coy way with which fierce beasts belie their fierceness. After some time of this the wolf started off at an easy lope in a manner that plainly showed he was going somewhere. He made it clear to Buck that he was to come, and they ran side by side through the somber twilight, straight up the creek bed, into the gorge from which it issued, and across the bleak divide where it took its rise.

On the opposite slope of the watershed they came down into a level country where were great stretches of forest and many streams, and through these great stretches they ran steadily, hour after hour, the sun rising higher and the day growing warmer. Buck was wildly glad. He knew he was at last answering the call, running by the side of his wood brother toward the place from where the call surely came. Old memories were coming upon him fast, and he was stirring to them as of old he stirred to the realities of which they were the shadows. He had done this thing before, somewhere in that other and dimly remembered world, and he was doing it again, now, running free in the open, the unpacked earth underfoot, the wide sky overhead. ❖

In the following excerpt, a young girl named Karana is alone on an island after all the members of her tribe leave. In this section, Karana tries to leave the island for the mainland.

from **Island of the Blue Dolphins** by Scott O'Dell

At dusk I looked back. The Island of the Blue Dolphins had disappeared. This was the first time that I felt afraid.

There were only hills and valleys of water around me now. When I was in a valley I could see nothing and when the canoe rose out of it, only the ocean stretching away and away. Night fell and I drank from the basket. The water cooled my throat.

The sea was black and there was no difference between it and the sky. The waves made no sound among themselves, only faint noises as they went under the canoe or struck against it. Sometimes the noises seemed angry and at other times like people laughing. I was not hungry because of my fear.

© GREAT SOURCE. COPYING IS PROHIBITED.

The first star made me feel less afraid. It came out low in the sky and it was in front of me, toward the east. Other stars began to appear all around, but it was this one I kept my gaze upon. It was in the figure that we call a serpent, a star which shone green and which I knew. Now and then it was hidden by mist, yet it always came out brightly again. Without this star I would have been lost, for the waves never changed. They came always from the same direction and in a manner that kept pushing me away from the place I wanted to reach. For this reason the canoe made a path in the black water like a snake. But somehow I kept moving toward the star which shone in the east. ❖

✳ What style choices did Jack London and Scott O'Dell make? Use the chart below to compare and contrast their styles. Under the authors' names, give specific examples from the two excerpts.

Style Choice	Jack London	Scott O'Dell
Point of View (who is telling the story)		
Length of sentences		
Type of language (formal or informal, simple or complex)		
Use of figurative language (imagery, similes and metaphors)		
Tone (how the writing sounds: suspenseful, scary, exciting, and so on)		

You are now ready to write the first draft of your essay.

© GREAT SOURCE. COPYING IS PROHIBITED.

Imagine you are on a planning committee for next year's seventh-grade English class. Based on the excerpts, which book—*The Call of the Wild* or *Island of the Blue Dolphins*—do you think should be required reading? Why? You may choose the criteria on which you base your answer, but consideration of style should be one of your points. Other criteria might be subject matter, compelling story, action, description, and so on. Remember, it is not enough to say you just liked one better. You need to explain why.

✳ Meet with your partner or group to share the first draft of your paper. Before you read each other's papers, it is important for you to know what your teacher will look for when he or she reads your story.

An outstanding paper will

✳ tell which book you would recommend.

✳ explain why you recommend that book by dealing with a comparison of important features such as style, subject matter, plot, and description.

✳ show how well you are able to

  ▪ express your ideas

  ▪ organize your ideas

  ▪ write clear sentences that flow when read aloud

  ▪ make good word choices (specific nouns, vivid verbs)

  ▪ spell words correctly

  ▪ punctuate and capitalize correctly

✳ Each of you will now read your paper aloud to a partner or members of a small group. When each person finishes reading, the other members should tell the reader what they liked about the paper. Then they should use the criteria in the box to offer constructive criticism. As your group members talk about your paper, make notes so that when you revise it, you will remember what they suggested.

Reading your paper with your group will help you make decisions about what you want to revise.

© GREAT SOURCE. COPYING IS PROHIBITED.

Reread the list of the traits of an outstanding paper in Lesson 34. Then, using your notes, go over your draft carefully to decide how you can improve it. Make a clean copy of the final draft of your paper. Remember to give it a title.

REFLECTION

As you have worked through the lessons in this book, you have had many opportunities to learn and practice skills and strategies to become a better reader and writer. You have learned and practiced five essential critical reading and writing strategies:

- interacting with the text
- making connections
- exploring multiple perspectives
- focusing on language and craft
- studying an author

In this reflection, consider how much you have improved as a reader and writer during your work with the *Daybook*. Think about the areas in which you need more practice to become a more effective and confident reader and writer.

✳ Write a paragraph reflecting on how you have improved and what you can do to become a stronger reader and writer.

_____

_____

_____

_____

_____

_____

_____

_____

_____

Self-assessment is an important part of learning how to strengthen your reading and writing skills.

© GREAT SOURCE. COPYING IS PROHIBITED.

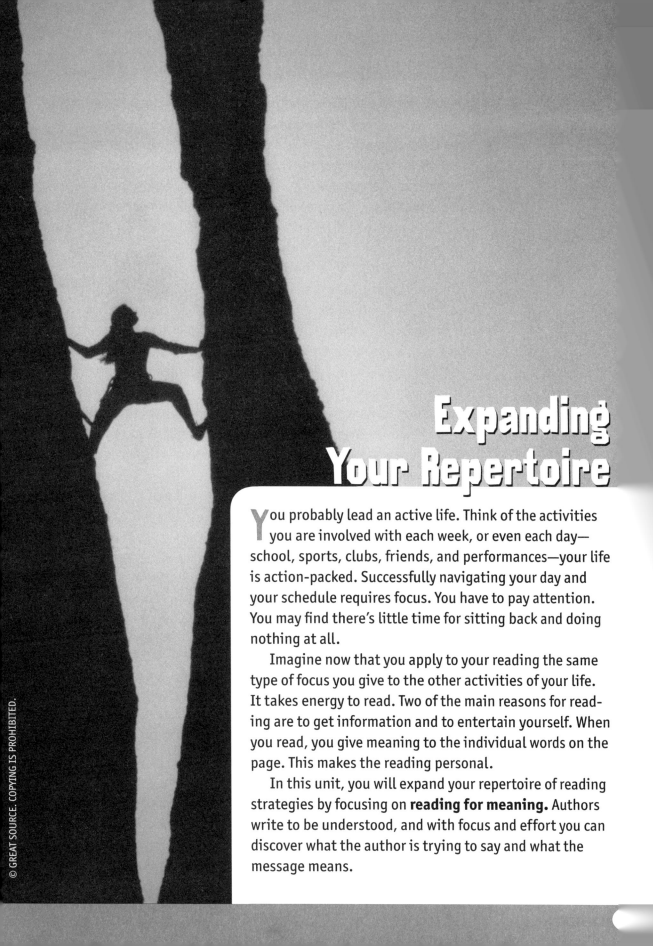

© GREAT SOURCE. COPYING IS PROHIBITED.

Expanding Your Repertoire

You probably lead an active life. Think of the activities you are involved with each week, or even each day—school, sports, clubs, friends, and performances—your life is action-packed. Successfully navigating your day and your schedule requires focus. You have to pay attention. You may find there's little time for sitting back and doing nothing at all.

Imagine now that you apply to your reading the same type of focus you give to the other activities of your life. It takes energy to read. Two of the main reasons for reading are to get information and to entertain yourself. When you read, you give meaning to the individual words on the page. This makes the reading personal.

In this unit, you will expand your repertoire of reading strategies by focusing on **reading for meaning.** Authors write to be understood, and with focus and effort you can discover what the author is trying to say and what the message means.

Imagine two baseball teams in the middle of a game: the pitcher on the mound, watching the catcher's signs; the shortstop hunched over, glove in hand and the batter watching the pitcher. Everyone is interacting. But team sports are not the only games that involve interaction—think of your favorite board game or video game. Even these, like baseball, require that players pay attention to details in order to form winning strategies. Each move a player makes is determined by an earlier move. In all of these cases, the participants must **interact** with the game in order to play it effectively.

Interacting with a text also requires strategy. Instead of players on a field, there are words on a page; rather than characters on a screen, the words come to life in your mind. Your job is to pay attention and to make meaning from the words.

Interacting with the text requires you to establish *what* is happening, *when* and *where* it is happening, *why* it is happening, and *who* it is happening to. As you read the following excerpt from the novel *Ice Drift* by Theodore Taylor, use your **Response Notes** to record important details about *who, what, when, where,* and *why* as you best determine them in a very brief moment in the novel.

from **Ice Drift** by Theodore Taylor

Response
Notes

What does this mean?

The time was mid-October 1868, on the (eve of the long winter darkness.) The shallow noon light was already fading. Snow had fallen a week earlier and would stay until almost June. The caribou were mating, char were spawning, and the sea ice was forming. All over the arctic, inhabitants, both human and animal, were preparing for the frozen siege.

✳ Interacting with the text requires you to focus on *who* is involved and what you are learning about the characters. As you continue reading, use your **Response Notes** to record details about the *who* in the novel.

Jamka, the lead sledge dog, had sniffed out the small hole where he expected a ringed seal would soon surface to breathe, and Alika had prepared for the day's hunt by building a windbreak of snow blocks and a snow-block seat next to the *aglus* that he covered with a square of polar bear hide to keep his

© GREAT SOURCE. COPYING IS PROHIBITED.

bottom warm. An indicator rod of caribou bone was in the hole. When a seal came up, it might touch the thin rod, wiggling it and alerting him.

Descendants of the Thule people who had first settled in the north a thousand years before, fourteen-year-old Alika and his brother, ten-year-old Sulu, were Inuit, meaning "mankind," and their diet was mostly from the sea, mostly cooked.

Alika said to Jamka. "You promised me a seal a long time ago."

The Greenland husky, dark eyes always seeming to have an intelligent expression, stared back as if to say, "But I didn't tell you when."

Alika sighed.

When Alika was seven years old, he and Jamka had bonded in an emergency, and they had been almost inseparable ever since. One September day, when the ice was still thin on a lake two miles from Nunatak, Alika was fishing for char when the crust broke. Into the water he went. Jamka pulled him out by the parka hood and dragged him home. Alika well remembered looking up at Jamka's wet belly as he slid on his back along the snow. He was convinced that Jamka thought like a human, and he trusted the dog with his life.

✳ Interacting with the text requires that you keep track of what is going on. Remember, you are reading for meaning. Use your **Response Notes** to keep track of what is happening.

Alika rose and called to the other dogs that were half buried in the snow. It was past time to go home.

Jamka stood up, also looking at the quickly darkening, threatening sky. Very experienced, Jamka seemed to sense danger in guiding the team, as if he knew exactly where hidden crevasses were; where the thin ice was. He'd fought polar bears and been wounded by them. He was the best lead dog Kussu had ever owned.

Then suddenly, unexpectedly, the floe shook and a loud crack shattered the stillness. Alika watched in horror as the dark expanse of water between the ice floe and the shore began to widen. *Three feet! Five feet! Seven feet!* Alika's body stiffened with fear and helplessness. The same thing had happened to several villagers without kayaks to reach shore. Their floe had split off, and they were never seen again. ❖

Now that you have interacted with the text, think about what you have learned so far.

© GREAT SOURCE. COPYING IS PROHIBITED.

✳ Use the chart below to organize your thinking about what you know and what you don't understand.

What is going on?	What don't I understand?
It's winter and very cold.	Why will snow stay until June? Is the Arctic always cold?

✳ Another way to monitor your understanding is to try to step into what you are reading and "walk around" in the action and events. In the space below, write the next paragraph in the story. Predict what will happen next.

_____

_____

_____

_____

_____

_____

_____

_____

_____

_____

_____

Interacting with the text requires that you pay attention to what is going on, give meaning to what you read, and monitor your understanding as you read.

© GREAT SOURCE. COPYING IS PROHIBITED.

As a reader, you are a very important player in the text. That's right. Even though you may not be the narrator, a character, or the author, you are involved. Sometimes what we read helps us understand ourselves better. Other times, we learn about other people and understand them better. Your knowledge and experience bring the story to life and allow the words on the page to become the ideas in your head.

Great writers are experts at creating people and situations that remind us of ourselves. Although we might not identify with everything a character does, we often see a little of ourselves or someone we know in the hopes, actions, and fears the author writes about.

In the following excerpt from *True Believer* by Virginia Euwer Wolff, look for something of yourself in the character, LaVaughn. Or perhaps the events and situations remind you of a friend or a family member instead. Use your **Response Notes** to keep track of places in the story where you **make connections.**

from **True Believer** by Virginia Euwer Wolff

Response Notes

31.

On Saturday night
I watched my mom making herself too pretty,
too detailed for just a night out with those women
she takes the job stress off with once in a while.
They go to a movie, a real laugher, and they howl together,
or a real crier, and they sob together,
and they have Chinese food after,
and they make a fuss over the movie for hours,
changing the ending to make it better, or even the middle,
till I wonder why they saw it in the first place.
Once I went along. But their voices
were too drowning out for me.

But this night my mom is not just
going with those women, I could tell.
It wasn't just pants and old shoes and a jacket.
It was a dress.

My mom can really wear a dress.

Something was up.

© GREAT SOURCE. COPYING IS PROHIBITED.

33.

His name is Lester.
He is at her new job, he is in charge of something there.
And he is coming to our house to eat supper.
My mom is a good cook, she brags
she never has those packages like at Jolly's house.
"Things with sauce" she calls them
and she insists, "We need sauce, I'll make sauce."
Now Lester is coming and I'll see what he looks like.

I still have my mind on Jody
And it's hard to concentrate on the rest of life
And now we get Lester. My throat goes lumpy.

My mom tells me to climb on the kitchen stool
and get down the good plates, three of them,
plus three more for dessert plus one for the rolls.
She tells me to move the stool to the other cupboard
to get the glasses we only use on holidays
when the aunts are here.

This Lester has some special stomach
to need all these special plates and holidays glasses.
Is it because he has a good job?
Is it because my mom is lonely?
I'm lonely, and I eat on the regular plates
every single time.

"Oh, and La Vaughn, you'll wear something nice, won't you?
How about that green sweater with pretty stitching?"
I honestly believe I hear my mom cooing.
Ick.
It makes me queasy.

I sit on the stool and tear up the lettuce
wondering what will happen
and resenting dressing up for Lester
when it's Jody I dress for everyday,
all the time sneaking and hiding from wherever he might be
to make sure he won't see me.

It's just a mouth.
Two mouths.
Jody's mouth and mine.
Just mouths, that's all.
Just the thought can take me out of whatever room I'm in.

© GREAT SOURCE. COPYING IS PROHIBITED.

34.

Lester arrives in person,
he is carrying live flowers in paper.
I feel bad immediately for my grudge on him.
He leans forward, he shakes my hand, his hand is soft.

My mom exclaims so bright over the flowers
and tells me almost in a song voice
to get the blue patterned ceramic pot and put them in.
Only she says "arrange," not put.

If Lester could read minds
he would see the history going between my mom and me.
That blue patterned pot
was a wedding gift. She always keeps it on that shelf
and it is sacred. ❖

✳ Two of the main characters in this section are LaVaughn and her mother. Try to think of instances in the story when one of these characters reminds you of yourself or some part of your own experience. How do the characters remind you of people you know well? How do they and the situation LaVaughn describes make you feel?

Example from the story: _when her mother goes out with her friends for a movie or_
Chinese food.

Makes me feel: _like my mother should do more of that. She works too hard and needs_
to enjoy herself more.

Example from the story: _____

_____

Makes me feel: _____

_____

Example from the story: _____

_____

Makes me feel: _____

_____

> Connecting the characters
> to your own experiences helps
> you understand yourself and
> the text better.

© GREAT SOURCE. COPYING IS PROHIBITED.

Each single moment in time is unique for each person. Each moment of your life is shaped by where you are and what you are doing. Think about a recent significant event. Maybe it was the birth of a new cousin, or the death of an older relative; maybe it was a natural disaster in a far-off place. Think about what you were doing at that moment. Now think about what that moment might have been like for someone who was personally involved.

Multiple perspectives allow a reader to look at a moment or event from more than one angle. From each **point of view,** the reader gains insight. In the following two excerpts from the same novel, you will see how an author weaves a moment together from two different perspectives.

Begin by reading Billy's perspective of the events. Use your **Response Notes** to record your reactions and questions.

Response Notes

from **The Terrorist** by Caroline Cooney

Once on the train, none of them sat. It would be unthinkable to take a seat when you could stand by the doors, swaying, feet spread, refusing to hold a metal post and too short to reach a hanging strap. Billy prided himself on never having fallen into anybody.

He gazed with superiority at the businessmen and women whose brief-cases were hugged between their knees. Leather cases always made him think of his family's arrival at Heathrow Airport. Signs everywhere said not to leave baggage unattended. "Are they worried somebody will steal my pajamas?" Billy had asked his father.

"No, they're worried about bombs," explained his father. "Terrorists."

Billy's mother was so horrified by that, she reacted like a shepherd whose flock is surrounded by wolves. Constantly watching their dozen suitcases and tugging to make the pile more compact, she eyed innocent strangers for signs of evil intent.

Billy yearned to abandon a suitcase and see what happened next. Either Scotland Yard or MI 5 would seize it, which would be worth the whole flight, or else a terrorist would steal it and Billy could seize the terrorist, which would be worth any two flights.

Annoyingly, his parents had refused to leave a suitcase.

The train pulled into Baker Street, where they would change lines. The three boys hurled themselves out into the belowground corridors and sets of stairs.

© GREAT SOURCE. COPYING IS PROHIBITED.

A train was waiting, doors open, car packed. They crammed themselves in. No need to hang on to anything this time: other bodies would keep them upright.

At the third stop, they leaped from the car, and began the race to see who would get outside to the fresh air first. It was another five pence for the winner. Billy firmly believed that pennies added up, even British pennies.

But he got caught by passengers swarming onto the train, so Chris and Georgie got way ahead. Chris yelled triumphantly over his shoulder, "I'm gonna win this time!"

Billy sprinted after them, slithering among the Indians, Asians, and Africans who made up the English population that he had thought would look like Robin Hood and Maid Marian.

Passengers funneled toward the only working escalator. Tired people stood on the right side, clutching briefcases, handbags, and shopping trolleys, little wire suitcases on wheels that Londoners used to bring their groceries home. Energetic people ran up the left edge as the steps moved under their feet.

Chris and Georgie were almost out of sight.

Billy tried to elbow past some old ladies, but somebody caught his arm. Expecting to be yelled at, Billy prepared to hide his American accent. Billy didn't mind being yelled at, but he hated it when somebody inevitable muttered, "Oh, those rowdy American children!"

If there was one thing English children were not, it was rowdy. Sometimes Billy wondered if they were even alive.

Actually at London International Academy, he was in classes with every nationality *except* the English. They had their own schools to go to. He was living right here in England and had tons of friends and none of them were English.

Billy decided on another new page in his notebook. He'd have a Nationality List. A Country Collection. Just in his sixth-grade homeroom were kids from Denmark, Iran, Syria, Argentina, Israel, Hong Kong, and America. He was pretty sure Juan was from somewhere else entirely, and Priya might be from India.

But the man who caught his arm actually smiled, saying, "Your friend dropped this."

Billy was amazed and pleased by this unusual helpfulness. "Oh gee, thanks a lot," he said. He grabbed the package and tore up the escalator.

Stopped by a woman who was awkwardly balancing a stroller with a baby across the width of the rising stairs, he glanced down at the package.

Funny.

He didn't remember Georgie or Chris carrying anything. Just book bags slung on their shoulders.

There was something very British about the package.

Not American.

The whole way it was wrapped. The cheapness of the cellophane tape. The texture of the brown paper.

© GREAT SOURCE. COPYING IS PROHIBITED.

He remembered the signs and warnings at Heathrow. Do Not Leave Any Luggage Unattended. He remembered the fire drills at school, which the big kids said were really bomb drills.

There was a sickening moment of knowledge.

He could not throw the package into the innocent crowd.

There was no place to set it down.

Nor could he give it back.

In front of him was a sleeping baby.

Oh, Mom! thought Billy, turning away from the stroller and wrapping himself around the package.

The package exploded. ✤

✳ Take a moment to think about your strongest images and reactions to this scene. What are your impressions of Billy? What is the strongest image in your mind of what he is seeing and feeling throughout this scene? Do a quick-write to get all your thoughts and reactions down on paper.

_____

_____

_____

_____

_____

_____

_____

_____

_____

_____

_____

_____

_____

_____

_____

_____

© GREAT SOURCE. COPYING IS PROHIBITED.

✳ Now read another section of the novel that tells about the same moment in time, but from Billy's sister's **perspective.** Use your **Response Notes** to keep track of where you see similarities and differences in Billy's and Laura's perspectives.

Laura often thought that when her brother, Billy, grew up, he was going to be the heartthrob of his entire school. You could see in his arms the muscles that were going to come. And his thick, dark hair, which he never combed or brushed after a shower (assuming you could shove him into a shower with the water on in the first place), was going to lie around on his forehead, and girls would want to sweep it away from his flirty eyes…

Laura loved London. She was from a small suburb and, like everybody else in America, considered a car the only way to move, and she was correct: at home, public transportation was a trial and a joke. But in London she could hop on a bus, take the tube, or flag down a taxi. From Shakespeare to sweat-shirt shopping, she was free the way no kids at home were until they had their own car.

The 113 appeared with Eddie waving insanely.

She got on, said "Hi" to Eddie and three other L.I.A. students, and the five of them sorted out with whom they would have lunch, whether anybody was going on the London Walk that afternoon, and had Laura heard about the escaped terrorists?

At L.I.A., they had bomb practice, the way in Massachusetts they had fire drills. L.I.A. students marched out the door and lined up on the sidewalk while London police timed them and teachers checked lockers and possible bomb-hiding spots. Everybody was happy, especially the people who got out of math…

"No, I didn't hear anything," said Laura. "What terrorists?" She wondered how the embassies would handle privacy once *Caller I.D.* appeared in London.

The five teenagers changed buses. They were disgusted with Laura. Hadn't she watched the morning news? Hadn't she read the morning paper?…

The bus halted with a lurch at their stop, which was in front of the tube exit and a mere three-block walk to L.I.A.

Laura was thinking that maybe terrific blond Andrew (a Ten) would talk to her after history. Maybe in the cafeteria she'd finally be in line next to that splendid hunk Mohammed (as opposed to Muhamet, who was sleazy, and Mohammet, who dated Jenny), and then—

Ambulances and fire trucks filled the sidewalks.

People were screaming and sobbing.

Police and teachers from L.I.A. were rushing back and forth

Her friends—Andrew, Con, Mohammed, Jehran, Bethany—were clinging to one another.

© GREAT SOURCE. COPYING IS PROHIBITED.

What had happened? Who was hurt? It must be very bad, it must be somebody from school, it must be—

Laura's clothing shivered on top of her skin.

Billy took the Underground.

Billy could be such a jerk. He liked to play with the car doors. He'd stick his head out, or his foot, and yank himself back in the nick of time. Laura was always yelling at him.

But of course it couldn't be Billy, because Billy was the kind of person who survived. Billy would always land on his feet. ❖

✴ You probably noticed several parallel events in time, and yet Laura is focusing her attention on very different things than Billy was. Use the space below to compare the images, ideas, and actions that contribute to their different perspectives of the same period of time. Refer back to your **Response Notes.**

Billy	Laura
✳ Billy gets on the subway with his friends.	✳ Laura is still waiting for the bus.
✳ Billy is thinking about the businessmen and focuses on their leather briefcases.	✳ Laura is thinking about Billy as a person.

✴ Compare your chart with a partner. Discuss how reading the two different perspectives affected your reactions to the events. Why or why not is it an effective technique to give more than one perspective?

_____

_____

_____

_____

_____

Exploring multiple perspectives allows you to gain additional insight and understanding.

© GREAT SOURCE. COPYING IS PROHIBITED.

One of the ways authors appeal to readers is through the language they choose. **Emotional language** can evoke feelings. You might feel angry or scared or happy after reading a passage. The words and phrases can evoke strong mental pictures.

Read the excerpt that follows. Use your **Response Notes** to keep track of ideas that appeal to your emotions. Circle words and phrases or sentences that cause particular reactions.

from "**Homeless**" by Anna Quindlen

Her name was Ann, and we met in the Port Authority Bus Terminal several Januarys ago. I was doing a story on homeless people. She said I was wasting my time talking to her, she was just passing through, although she'd been passing through for more than two weeks. To prove to me that this was true, she rummaged through a tote bag and a manila envelope and finally unfolded a sheet of typing paper and brought out her photographs.

They were not pictures of family, or friends, or even a dog or cat, its eyes brown-red in the flashbulb's light. They were pictures of a house. It was like a thousand houses in a hundred towns, not suburb, not city, but somewhere in between, with aluminum siding and a chain link fence, a narrow driveway running up to a one-car garage and a patch of backyard. The house was yellow. I looked on the back for a date or a name, but neither was there. There was no need for discussion. I knew what she was trying to tell me, for it was something I had often felt. She was not adrift, alone, anonymous, although her bags and her raincoat with the grime shadowing its creases had made me believe she was. She had a house, or at least once upon a time had had one. Inside were curtains, a couch, a stove, pot holders. You are where you live. She was somebody.

I've never been very good at looking at the big picture, taking the global view, and I've always been a person with an overactive sense of place, the legacy of an Irish grandfather. So it is natural that the thing that seems most wrong with the world to me right now is that there are so many people with no homes. I'm not simply talking about shelter from the elements, or three square meals a day or a mailing address to which the welfare people can send the check—although I know that all these are important for survival. I'm talking about a home, about precisely those kinds of feelings that have wound up in cross-stitch and French knots on samplers over the years. ❖

I don't always think of homeless people as "somebody."

© GREAT SOURCE. COPYING IS PROHIBITED.

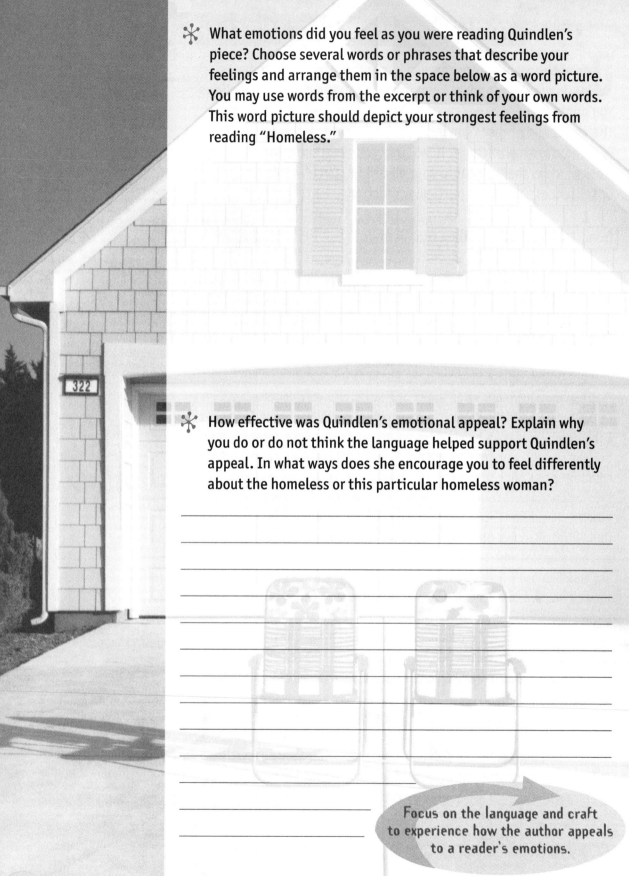

✳ What emotions did you feel as you were reading Quindlen's piece? Choose several words or phrases that describe your feelings and arrange them in the space below as a word picture. You may use words from the excerpt or think of your own words. This word picture should depict your strongest feelings from reading "Homeless."

✳ How effective was Quindlen's emotional appeal? Explain why you do or do not think the language helped support Quindlen's appeal. In what ways does she encourage you to feel differently about the homeless or this particular homeless woman?

Focus on the language and craft to experience how the author appeals to a reader's emotions.

© GREAT SOURCE. COPYING IS PROHIBITED.

The meaning you get from your reading determines how you react to what you read. What are some reasons that you were drawn to the writing of one author more than another in this unit? Discuss this with a partner.

In this lesson, you will analyze the meaning you took from each excerpt as a way of thinking about your reaction to each author. Each writes about a different subject with flair and style. But the work you did *with* the author determines what you will take away. By *monitoring* your reading of each author, you will figure out why that author appeals to you.

❋ Use the chart below to help you sort out the meaning you took from each piece. In each box, answer the questions asked.

Author	Did you make a personal connection to this piece? Why or why not?	What did you notice about the language and craft in this writing?	What did you learn from this author?
Theodore Taylor, *Ice Drift*			
Virginia Euwer Wolff, "True Believer"			
Caroline Cooney, *The Terrorist*			
Anna Quindlen, "Homeless"			

© GREAT SOURCE. COPYING IS PROHIBITED.

✳ Now think about what you can learn from the author that will be useful in your own writing. Use Cooney's crafting of multiple perspectives as a guide, for example. Think of an event in your life that can be told from two different viewpoints. Use the space below to outline the events from each viewpoint, just as you did when you charted Billy's and Laura's perspectives.

Viewpoint #1	Viewpoint #2

✳ Using the chart above, draft an opening paragraph from each perspective. Share your paragraphs with a partner.

PARAGRAPH #1

_____

_____

_____

_____

_____

_____

_____

PARAGRAPH #2

_____

_____

_____

_____

_____

_____

One way of studying an author is to monitor the connections and meaning you make from reading that author's work.

© GREAT SOURCE. COPYING IS PROHIBITED.

© GREAT SOURCE. COPYING IS PROHIBITED.

Interacting with the Text

We are surrounded by **visual information**, some designed to entertain and some designed to persuade. Knowing how words and pictures work together to communicate messages will help you understand and question the content of the messages. To **interact** with **visual text**, you can use many of the strategies you have already learned for interacting with print text. You will also learn new strategies for reading visual images, and you will create visual text of your own.

Readers **make inferences** by reading "between the lines," filling in what is not stated directly by making a reasonable guess that is based on what is stated. You use what you read in a text and what you know to make an inference. When you read dialogue in a story, you might put yourself in the character's place. When the text includes visual information, you are given additional clues as to how a character feels and speaks the words in the story, similar to stage directions in a play.

Response Notes

Bone is a nine-volume series that tells the epic adventures of the three Bone cousins—Fone, Smiley, and Phoney. They are run out of Boneville, get separated in an uncharted desert, and slowly find each other again in a forested valley populated by strange and wonderful creatures. Thorn rescues and befriends Fone. She hopes to help him find his cousins and then send them all home, but there are terrifying adventures ahead that will interfere with their plans. In the excerpt that follows, Thorn and Fone go to the spring fair. As you read the story, see what you can infer about the characters.

© GREAT SOURCE. COPYING IS PROHIBITED.

© GREAT SOURCE. COPYING IS PROHIBITED.

✳ Use the inference chart to record your conclusions about the characters and the story. In the right-hand column describe or draw the word and visual clues writer/artist Jeff Smith provided. There is space for you to add another inference and other techniques.

Inference	Technique
Fone Bone has a crush on Thorn.	hearts around his word bubble dreamy-eyed look created by adding a line at the top of his eyes
Thorn is protective of Fone Bone.	She holds his hand and leads him. She defends him against Tom's insult.

Reading the pictures and the text together helps you make better inferences about the story.

© GREAT SOURCE. COPYING IS PROHIBITED.

One way of understanding a **genre,** or a type of writing, is to look at its **characteristics.** Characteristics are the features that define a genre. In fantasy, for example, you might find talking animals or a battle between good and evil. Visual texts have their own characteristics, such as ways to show emotion or emphasis. Knowing the characteristics can help you get more out of a text.

As you finish reading the scene with Thorn, Tom, and Fone Bone at the fair, think about the characteristics of **graphic novels**.

from **Bone** by Jeff Smith

Response Notes

© GREAT SOURCE. COPYING IS PROHIBITED.

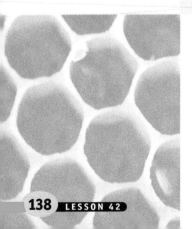

* Before you write about the characteristics of this genre, think about the inferences you made about the characters in Lesson 41. What do you you think about them now? What will they do next?

© GREAT SOURCE. COPYING IS PROHIBITED.

✳ To help you think about characteristics of visual texts, answer the following questions.

■ In what order did you read the panels of *Bone*?

_____

_____

_____

_____

_____

■ Where is Fone Bone placed in relationship to Tom and Thorn in this scene compared to the panels in Lesson 41? How much power does he seem to have to separate Tom and Thorn?

_____

_____

_____

_____

_____

_____

■ What are the different ways that Smith uses lines to show anger?

_____

_____

_____

_____

_____

_____

> Sequence, layout, and expression lines are three characteristics of graphic art that convey meaning.

© GREAT SOURCE. COPYING IS PROHIBITED.

Artists who write and illustrate **graphic novels** use such elements as lines, depth of field, and space to convey their ideas. The choices artists make about the design of the visual images contribute to their individual **styles**.

In *The Borden Tragedy,* Rick Geary presents the story of Lizzie Borden, who was accused of using an axe to kill her father and stepmother in 1892. Although she was ultimately found not guilty, suspicion remained, especially since the murderer was never found. Geary claims that his story has been "excerpted and adapted from the unpublished memoirs of a (thus far) unknown lady of Fall River, Massachusetts." As you read about Lizzie's visit to Alice Russell on the night before the murders, pay attention to the art as well as the words.

from **The Borden Tragedy** by Rick Geary

© GREAT SOURCE. COPYING IS PROHIBITED.

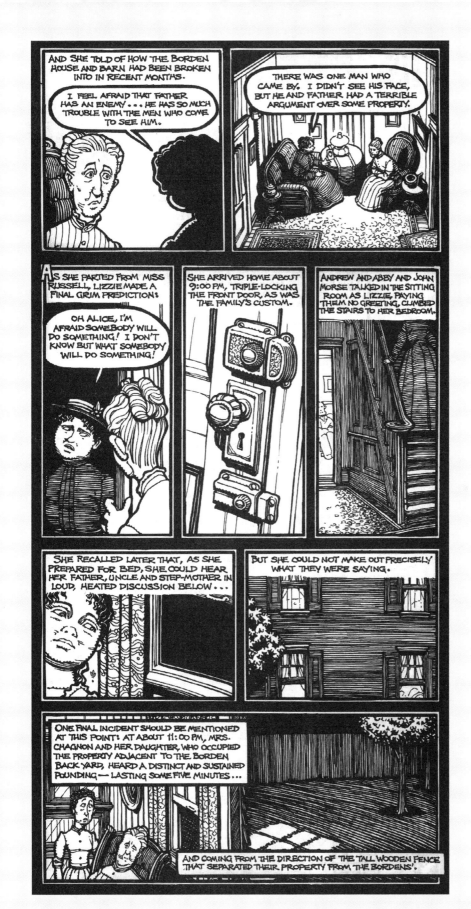

© GREAT SOURCE. COPYING IS PROHIBITED.

✳ Use the following chart to compare the design of the panels in *The Borden Tragedy* to the panels in *Bone*.

	The Borden Tragedy	Bone
Kinds of lines and how they are used		
Depth of field (impression of depth, having a foreground and a background)	Art seems 3-dimensional. The characters stand out from the background.	
Use of space		Each panel includes a lot of detail. There is often some white space near the center, where nothing is drawn.

✳ Compare Jeff Smith's style in *Bone* to Rick Geary's in *The Borden Tragedy*. Which style do you prefer? Why? Use the chart to support your thinking.

_____

_____

_____

_____

_____

_____

_____

Authors and artists create a distinctive style, which determines how the reader experiences their work.

© GREAT SOURCE. COPYING IS PROHIBITED.

44 LESSON

Where do the words go in graphic novels? You have already seen two techniques for placing words in a visual text. Jeff Smith used just **dialogue** in word balloons. His word balloons take on different shapes, such as the wavy boundary around "Hello, small mammal!" and the hearts around the first part of Fone Bone's conversation with Thorn. These details help the author convey a character's feelings. Rick Geary used both a **narrator**, whose words are not in a balloon, and dialogue in word balloons for Alice and Lizzie. The word balloons seem almost formal with their similar shape and dark lines, which would fit the atmosphere Geary was trying to re-create.

Sound also has to be conveyed visually. How does the reader know that a character is shouting or whispering? How does the reader know which words to emphasize or how fast or slow the character is speaking? How does the reader know when a speaker pauses?

✳ Imagine that you want to draw a conversation between two people. You can use the techniques that Jeff Smith and Rick Geary used, such as word balloons of different shapes, a bold font to emphasize certain words, and other techniques that you noticed.

Draw that conversation in the space provided on page 144. You can add drawings of characters, if you like, or you can let the word balloons stand alone. Readers of your conversation should be able to tell immediately how the two characters feel by looking at how their words are displayed.

© GREAT SOURCE. COPYING IS PROHIBITED.

© GREAT SOURCE. COPYING IS PROHIBITED.

Knowing how authors and artists convey dialogue, narration, and sound helps readers better understand both the art and the words in a visual text.

In *The Borden Tragedy,* Rick Geary claimed to be adapting a text that he had found. When artists adapt a text, they use the author's words and ideas and their own art. They may shorten the text or set it in a different time and place, but they do not significantly change the meaning of the original.

In this lesson, you will have a chance to adapt a poem by Edgar Allan Poe, "Annabel Lee." As you read or listen to the poem, visualize. Create pictures in your mind of the setting, of Annabel Lee, and of the speaker. You might even want to doodle in the **Response Notes**.

Annabel Lee by Edgar Allan Poe

Response
Notes

It was many and many a year ago,
In a kingdom by the sea,
That a maiden there lived whom you may know
By the name of Annabel Lee;
And this maiden she lived with no other thought
Than to love and be loved by me.

I was a child and she was a child,
In this kingdom by the sea:
But we loved with a love that was more than love—
I and my Annabel Lee—
With a love that the winged seraphs of heaven
Coveted her and me.

And this was the reason that, long ago,
In this kingdom by the sea,
A wind blew out of a cloud, chilling
My beautiful Annabel Lee;
So that her highborn kinsmen came
And bore her away from me,
To shut her up in a sepulcher
In this kingdom by the sea.

The angels, not half so happy in heaven,
Went envying her and me—
Yes!—that was the reason (as all men know,
In this kingdom by the sea)
That the wind came out of the cloud by night,
Chilling and killing my Annabel Lee.

Repeating love and loved—shows speaker's strong feelings

© GREAT SOURCE. COPYING IS PROHIBITED.

But our love it was stronger by far than the love
Of those who were older than we—
Of many far wiser than we—
And neither the angels in heaven above,
Nor the demons down under the sea,
Can ever dissever my soul from the soul
Of the beautiful Annabel Lee—

For the moon never beams, without bringing me dreams
Of the beautiful Annabel Lee;
And the stars never rise, but I feel the bright eyes
Of the beautiful Annabel Lee;
And so, all the night-tide, I lie down by the side
Of my darling—my darling—my life and my bride,
In the sepulcher there by the sea,
In her tomb by the sounding sea. ❖

✳ In the space below, plan your new visual text for the poem. Decide on the effect you want to achieve—humorous, solemn, "dark," "light," formal, informal, modern, and so on. Then select two techniques that were discussed in this unit that you could use. For example, do you want to use a narrator and dialogue or just the words of the poem? How much detail will be in the art? How much white space will you leave in your design?

✳ After you have made a plan, draw your visual poem on a separate sheet of paper. If you do not want to draw, you can use computer graphics or magazine cutouts for the visuals, as long as you can make them consistent with your intended effect.

A good way to understand how visual texts work is to create your own.

© GREAT SOURCE. COPYING IS PROHIBITED.

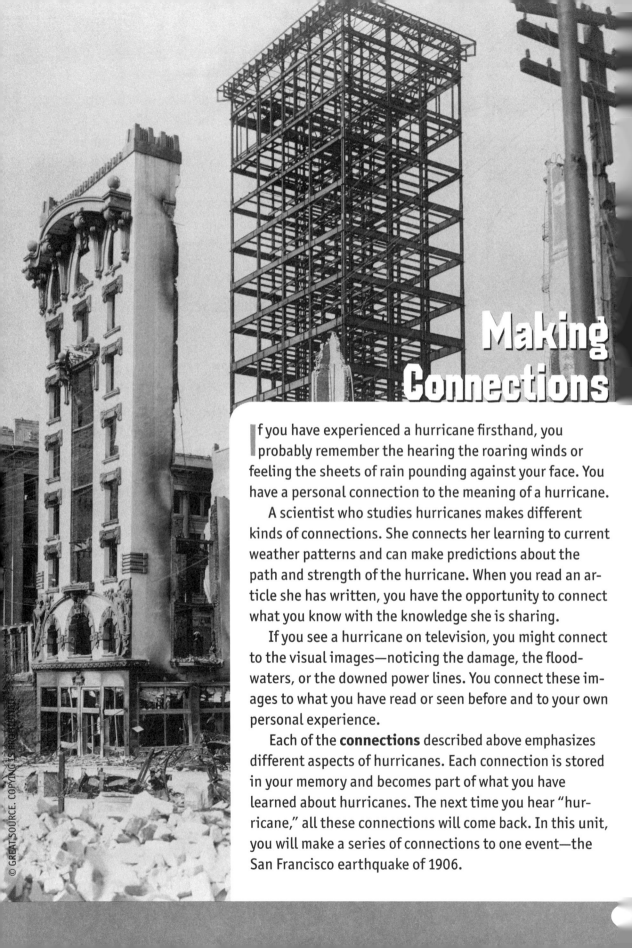

Making Connections

I f you have experienced a hurricane firsthand, you probably remember the hearing the roaring winds or feeling the sheets of rain pounding against your face. You have a personal connection to the meaning of a hurricane.

A scientist who studies hurricanes makes different kinds of connections. She connects her learning to current weather patterns and can make predictions about the path and strength of the hurricane. When you read an article she has written, you have the opportunity to connect what you know with the knowledge she is sharing.

If you see a hurricane on television, you might connect to the visual images—noticing the damage, the floodwaters, or the downed power lines. You connect these images to what you have read or seen before and to your own personal experience.

Each of the **connections** described above emphasizes different aspects of hurricanes. Each connection is stored in your memory and becomes part of what you have learned about hurricanes. The next time you hear "hurricane," all these connections will come back. In this unit, you will make a series of connections to one event—the San Francisco earthquake of 1906.

© GREAT SOURCE. COPYING IS PROHIBITED.

46

CONNECTING TO THE FACTS

Think for a moment about this scenario: A powerful city sits on the edge of the Pacific Ocean. The location gives it access to the sea and to other major cities. Think of a city with a fun-loving spirit—one filled with elegant hotels, opera, and theater. See hilly streets packed with tourists, traders, business operators, and immigrants. The narrow alleyways of Chinatown reveal restaurants, kite shops, and teahouses. But beneath the city, the earth trembles. Then it shifts. You probably know what will happen next.

As you read the following excerpt, circle information that confirms what you already know about earthquakes or about San Francisco. In your **Response Notes,** jot down surprises, record your questions, and list topics you want to discuss.

from **America's Great Disasters** by Martin W. Sandler

Response Notes

!!!

One of the things that we take for granted is the fact that the earth will remain solid and stable beneath our feet. When the earth begins to move violently and splits apart, those who are caught up in an earthquake experience a terror unlike any other.

Although it may be hard to believe, more than ten thousand earthquakes take place around the globe every year. Most are mild and go practically unnoticed. Some quakes are caused by the movement of the mixture of solid and liquid rock that lies under volcanoes. The most violent and most disastrous earthquakes, however, are those set into motion by movements that take place within the earth's "crust."

The crust is the layer of rock underneath the earth's soil. It contains many breaks, known as faults. The crust on either side of these faults moves very slowly. If two sections of crust become locked together and can't move, enormous pressure steadily mounts along that section of the fault. When the pressure is suddenly released by a shift of the crust on either side of the fault, it triggers a gigantic convulsion in the earth's surface, known as an earthquake . . . .

San Francisco, California, has been a city both blessed and cursed by its location. Perched on high hills overlooking the Pacific Ocean on one side and one of the world's loveliest harbors on the other, it is a beautiful place to live.

It is also a city that grew almost overnight. At the start of 1848, San Francisco was a tiny village containing about thirty-five houses. Its number of residents was so small that, according to one visitor, "not more than twenty-five persons would be seen in the streets at any one time."

© GREAT SOURCE. COPYING IS PROHIBITED.

Then, on January 24, 1848, gold was discovered in the area. People everywhere dropped whatever they were doing and headed for the goldfields, hoping to strike it rich. Most made the long journey by ship, landing in San Francisco's wide harbor.

As millions of gold-seekers and thousands of merchants, anxious to sell supplies, poured into San Francisco, its population exploded. Even after the goldfields had been mined dry, tens of thousands who had fallen in love with the region remained and settled there. By 1906, the once-tiny village had become a booming city of more than four hundred thousand people. . . .

But although few were aware of it at the time, the same physical location that made San Francisco so attractive to its residents, its growing number of visitors, and its businessmen also placed everyone in the city in great danger. Unfortunately for San Francisco, the city had sprung up within a few miles of one of the greatest hidden earth fractures in the world. Known as the San Andreas Fault, this break in the earth's crust runs parallel to the California coastline for about 800 miles. By 1906, pressure had been building up along the fault near San Francisco for years. Early in the morning of April 18, 1906, all this pressure finally erupted and unleashed the greatest earthquake America has ever experienced.

The quake began out at sea, some ninety miles north of San Francisco. Traveling southward at an incredible two miles per second, it tore up the coastline in its path and headed directly toward the city. It hit San Francisco at 5:13 A.M. ❖

✳ One way to monitor your connections is to think about what you learned through the reading. In the following chart, list some examples of information that is new to you.

What I Learned About San Francisco

1.

2.

3.

4.

5.

YOU

What I Learned About Earthquakes

1.

2.

3.

4.

5.

© GREAT SOURCE. COPYING IS PROHIBITED.

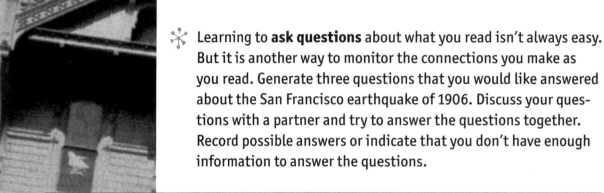

✳ Learning to **ask questions** about what you read isn't always easy. But it is another way to monitor the connections you make as you read. Generate three questions that you would like answered about the San Francisco earthquake of 1906. Discuss your questions with a partner and try to answer the questions together. Record possible answers or indicate that you don't have enough information to answer the questions.

Questions worth thinking about	Notes for possible answers	Need more information

✳ If you want to know more about a subject, you will probably have questions about it. Write a paragraph indicating what you would like to learn about the San Francisco earthquake that you didn't learn through your reading so far.

_____

_____

_____

_____

_____

_____

_____

_____

Connect what you already know to what you are learning or want to know.

 © GREAT SOURCE. COPYING IS PROHIBITED.

What if the focus of our attention shifts from the earthquake to the people who experienced it? An eyewitness provides a first-hand account. An eyewitness is someone who experiences an event and sees the effects of it. What did eyewitnesses feel and see?

Several eyewitness accounts follow. In your **Response Notes,** keep track of your reactions to what you learn from each person about the earthquake's effects on people's lives. Record questions that arise as you read.

from **America's Great Disasters** by Martin W. Sandler

Response Notes

Account #1: John Bartlett, a news editor: "Of a sudden," Bartlett later wrote, "we found ourselves staggering and reeling...then came the sickening sway of the earth that threw us flat upon our faces...We could not get on our feet. I looked in a dazed fashion around me...Big buildings were crumbling as one might crush a biscuit in one's hand...Storms of masonry rained into the street. Wild, high jangles of smashing glass cut a sharp note into the frightful roaring... Trolley tracks were twisted, their wires down, wriggling like serpents, flashing blue sparks all the time...From the south of us, faint, but all too clear came a horrible chorus of human cries of agony. Down there, in a ramshackle section of the city, the wretched houses had fallen in upon sleeping families..." ❖

from **Three Fearful Days** Malcolm Barker, editor

Account #2: James Hopper, a review writer:...I got up and walked to the window. I started to open it, but the pane obligingly fell outward and I poked my head out, the floor like a geyser beneath my feet. Then I heard the roar of bricks coming down in cataracts and the groaning of twisted girders all over the city, and at the same time I saw the moon, a calm, pale crescent in the green sky of dawn. Below it the skeleton frame of an unfinished sky-scraper was swaying from side to side with a swing as exaggerated and absurd as that of a palm in a stage tempest.

Just then the quake, with a sound as of a snarl, rose to its climax of rage, and the back wall of my building for three stories above me fell. I saw the mass pass across my vision swift as a shadow. It struck some little wooden houses in the alley below. I saw them crash in like emptied eggs and the bricks pass through the roof as through tissue paper.

The vibrations ceased and I began to dress. Then I noted the great silence. Throughout the long quaking, in this great house full of people I had not heard a

© GREAT SOURCE. COPYING IS PROHIBITED.

cry, not a sound, not a sob, not a whisper. And now, when the roar of crumbling buildings was over and only a brick was falling here and there like the trickle of a spent rain, this silence continued, and it was an awful thing. But now in the alley someone began to groan. It was a woman's groan, soft and low. ❖

Account #3: Harry Coleman, newspaper photographer: I saw miles of flames raging as smoke-blackened firemen stood helplessly by dry hydrants, watching their useless hoses curl up in the fire. With my cheeks almost blistered and my hair singed with the terrific heat, I shot pictures down Market Street past the Palace and Grand Hotels, through smoking canyons of red-hot twister girders, down to the wrecked ferry building, into Front Street and along the twisted rails of the Belt Line railroad, where the fire tugs Active and Leslie were pumping feeble streams of bay water on the roofs of wooden wharves, while excited seamen and stevedores trampled out sparks as they fell from the sky.

Threading my way over hot, cobbled streets, through swarms of stampeding rats, I continued my photographing up Mission Street into the lodging-house district, where great tongues of fire and clouds of smoke were everywhere, and the injured were trying to bandage each other's wounds with handkerchiefs and shreds of cloth. I pictured the frenzied crowds, standing aquiver, afraid to re-enter their houses to gather up what remained of their belongings. Frantic men separated from their families, pitiful mothers dragging frightened children, and sailors pulling sea-chests formed a human tide of refugees which flooded past my lens as they struggled toward the waterfront. ❖

Account #4: Mary Edith Griswold, assistant editor of *Sunset Magazine:* The fire is within two blocks of my house—everyone in my block had been told to leave. Our house has been ordered dynamited. The apathy of the last two days has given way. The firemen are frantic. If they don't stop the fire now the whole Western Addition will go—the policeman with a red face is running up and down in front of the house. A dead Italian lies in the middle of the street opposite my house. Members of his family sit around his body in a circle. I got so scared I couldn't swallow a glass of water. The heat on the balcony was intense—too hot to stay out there. The paint on the woodwork was blistering. Everyone was fire mad. My home will surely go. ❖

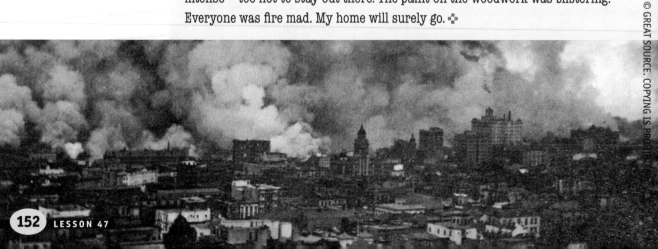

© GREAT SOURCE. COPYING IS PROHIBITED.

✳ Based on the connections you are making to the accounts of the earthquake, write a response to each question:

1 What would I do if I were in this situation?

_____

_____

2 What would be my greatest fear during the earthquake?

_____

_____

3 What would I do to help others during and after the earthquake?

_____

_____

✳ Now imagine that you have decided to head a relief effort to help the people who have survived the earthquake in San Francisco. On a separate sheet of paper, design a flier that is intended to recruit volunteers to support relief efforts in San Francisco. Use any details from the reading that will help convince people to support your cause.

Volunteer! Volunteer!
EARTHQUAKE RELIEF

 WE NEED VOLUNTEERS TO HELP THE PEOPLE WHO HAVE SURVIVED THE EARTHQUAKE IN SAN FRANCISCO.

SAN FRANCISCO
APR 1906
CALIFORNIA

Connect what people are feeling and experiencing to your feelings.

© GREAT SOURCE. COPYING IS PROHIBITED.

An eyewitness account can connect readers to an event. So can a fictional account.

Works of fiction often use places, events, and people from actual events. *Dragonwings* is a novel set in San Francisco in the early 1900s, and it depicts the 1906 earthquake. Moonshadow and his father are Chinese immigrants. In 1906, Chinatown was a newly developed neighborhood in San Francisco.

As you read, **connect** factual information you have learned about the events to the fictional account. In the **Response Notes,** keep track of any connections you make to information from Lessons 46 and 47.

from **Dragonwings** by Laurence Yep

Response Notes

I had gotten dressed and gone out to the pump to get some water. The morning was filled with that soft, gentle twilight of spring, when everything is filled with soft, dreamy colors and shapes; so when the earthquake hit, I did not believe it at first. It seemed like a nightmare where everything you take to be the rock-hard, solid basis for reality becomes unreal.

Wood and stone and brick and the very earth became fluidlike. The pail beneath the pump jumped and rattled like a spider dancing on a hot stove. The ground deliberately seemed to slide right out from under me. I landed on my back hard enough to drive the wind from my lungs. The whole world had become unglued, Our stable and Miss Whitlaw's house and the tenements to either side heaved and bobbed up and down, riding the ground like ships on a heavy sea. Down the alley mouth, I could see the cobblestone street undulate and twist like a red-backed snake.

From inside our stable, I could hear the cups and plates begin to rattle on their shelves, and the equipment on Father's worktable clattered and rumbled ominously.

Suddenly the door banged open and Father stumbled out with his clothes all in a bundle. "It's an earthquake, I think," he shouted. He had washed his hair the night before and had not had time to twist it into a queue, so it hung down his back long and black.

He looked around in the back yard. It was such a wide, open space that we were fairly safe there. Certainly more safe than in the frame doorway of our stable. He got into his pants and shirt and then his socks and boots.

"Do you think one of the mean dragons is doing all this?" I asked him.

"Maybe. Maybe not." Father had sat down to stuff his feet into his boots. "Time to wonder about that later. Now you wait here."

© GREAT SOURCE. COPYING IS PROHIBITED.

He started to get to his feet when the second tremor shook and he fell forward flat on his face. I heard the city bells ringing. They were rung by no human hand—the earthquake had just shaken them in their steeples. The second tremor was worse than the first. From all over came an immense wall of noise: of metal tearing, of bricks crashing, of wood breaking free from wood nails, and all. Everywhere, what man had built came undone. I was looking at a tenement house to our right and it just seemed to shudder and then collapse. One moment there were solid wooden walls and the next moment it had fallen with the cracking of wood and the tinkling of glass and the screams of people inside.

Mercifully, for a moment, it was lost to view in the cloud of dust that rose up. The debris surged against Miss Whitlaw's fence and toppled it over with a creak and a groan and a crash. I saw an arm sticking up from the mound of rubble and the hand was twisted at an impossible angle from the wrist. Coughing, Father pulled at my arm. "Stay here now," he ordered and started for Miss Whitlaw's.

✳ What is the strongest similarity or difference between this account and the ones you read in Lessons 46 and 47?

_____

_____

_____

✳ What are your feelings about Moonshadow's descriptions of the situation?

_____

_____

_____

_____

✳ Continue reading.

A strange, eerie silence hung over the city. The bells had stilled in their steeples, and houses had stopped collapsing momentarily. It was as if the city itself were holding its breath. Then we could hear the hissing of gas from the broken pipes, like dozens of angry snakes, and people, trapped inside the mounds, began calling. Their voices sounded faint and ghostly, as if dozens of ghosts floated over the rubble, crying in little, distant voices

© GREAT SOURCE. COPYING IS PROHIBITED.

Response Notes

for help. Robin and I pressed close to one another for comfort. It was Miss Whitlaw who saved us. It was she who gave us something important to do and brought us out of shock.

She pressed her lips together for a moment, as if she were deciding something. "We must get those people out."

"It would take four of us weeks to clear tunnels for them," Father said.

"We'll draft help. After all, we were put on this earth to help one another," Miss Whitlaw said.

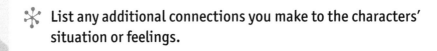

✳ **List any additional connections you make to the characters' situation or feelings.**

_____

_____

_____

✳ **As you continue reading, jot down any connections you make to the characters.**

We had gone to sleep on a street crowded with buildings, some three or four stories high and crowded with people; and now many of the houses were gone, and the ones that remained were dangerously close to falling too. There was a hole in the cobblestone street about a yard wide and twenty feet long. As we watched, a cobblestone fell over the edge, clattering ten feet to the bottom.

I heard one person compare it to being on the moon. It was that kind of desolate feeling—just looking at huge hills of rubble: of brick and broken wooden slats that had once been houses. On top of the piles we would see the random collection of things that had survived the quake: somebody's rag doll, an old bottle, a fiddle, the back of an upholstered chair . . . and a woman's slender wrist, sticking out of the rubble as if calling for help.

And then the survivors started to emerge, and I saw that there were as many hurt in mind as in body. Some people wandered out of the buildings almost naked, others still in their nightclothes. I saw one man with the lather on one side of his face, the other side already clean-shaven. In his hand was a lather-covered razor. One woman in a nightgown walked by, carrying her crying baby by its legs as if it were a dead chicken. Father caught her by the shoulder and gently took the baby from her.

"Fix her arms," Father told me. I set her arms so she could cradle the baby—as if the mother were a doll. Then Father put the baby back into her arms. She dumbly nodded her thanks and wandered on. ❖

© GREAT SOURCE. COPYING IS PROHIBITED.

✳ Another way of connecting is to imagine yourself as one of the characters in what you are reading. Imagine that you are the narrator Moonshadow. Take a minute to review what he is seeing and how he expresses his feelings about his situation. Then write the next scene in the novel as if you were Moonshadow.

_____
_____
_____
_____
_____
_____
_____
_____
_____
_____
_____
_____
_____
_____
_____
_____
_____
_____
_____
_____
_____
_____
_____
_____
_____

Connect to fictional accounts by comparing them to real events or by imagining yourself as one of the characters.

© GREAT SOURCE. COPYING IS PROHIBITED.

CONNECTING THROUGH PHOTOGRAPHS

In the novel *Dragonwings,* Moonshadow captures many of the images of the morning of the quake through the use of **descriptive language.** For example, he describes how the pail "jumped and rattled like a spider dancing on a hot stove."

In this lesson, you will examine two photographs and see how connecting to visual images enhances your understanding of the earthquake.

✳ Study the photograph closely. What images stand out for you? Begin by listing four phrases that *describe* what you see:

1 _____

2 _____

3 _____

4 _____

✳ Using at least eight descriptive words from your list, write a four-line poem that captures what you see in this photograph.

© GREAT SOURCE. COPYING IS PROHIBITED.

✳ Study this photo carefully. Take a few minutes to look closely for specific details. List three details that show what has happened as a result of the earthquake. For example, one detail might be:

Piles of broken bricks

My three details are

1 _____

2 _____

3 _____

What do these details remind you of? What are these details *like?* When you use *like,* you are making a connection between a detail and something it suggests to you. You probably remember that this connection is called a **simile.** Here's an example: *Splinters of wood are like bits of driftwood left by the tide.*

✳ Write a statement in the form of a simile for each of your three details. When you finish, share your similes with a partner.

1 _____

2 _____

3 _____

Connect to visual images by describing and drawing comparisons to them.

© GREAT SOURCE. COPYING IS PROHIBITED.

CONNECT TO INFORM FUTURE ACTIONS

You know that earthquakes can cause a great deal of damage. The shaking ground causes buildings and other structures to collapse. Fires result from broken gas and electric lines. In some cases, earthquakes cause fast-moving, giant ocean waves, called tsunamis, as the water heaves with the earth's movement. Extensive damage to property can result. Injuries to people and pets add to the destruction. All of the **connections** you've made in this unit focused on the reason earthquakes occur and the damage that results.

Let's focus now on connecting this knowledge of earthquakes and their results to how we can be better prepared for future earthquakes. The following excerpt is from one Red Cross website that details how to be prepared for an earthquake. In your **Response Notes,** mark with a star recommendations that you can put into effect fairly soon. Put a check beside recommendations that will take more time to implement.

Response Notes

"Safety Tips for Earthquakes" from the Rhode Island American Red Cross

PREPARE A HOME EARTHQUAKE PLAN

- Choose a safe place in every room—under a sturdy table or desk or against an inside wall where nothing can fall on you.

- Practice DROP, COVER, AND HOLD ON at least twice a year. Drop under a sturdy desk or table, hold on, and protect your eyes by pressing your face against your arm. If there's no table or desk nearby, sit on the floor against an interior wall away from windows, bookcases, or tall furniture that could fall on you. Teach children to DROP, COVER, AND HOLD ON!

- Choose an out-of-town family contact.

- Consult a professional to find out additional ways you can protect your home, such as bolting the house to its foundation and other structural mitigation techniques.

- Take a first aid class from your local Red Cross chapter. Keep your training current.

- Get training in how to use a fire extinguisher from your local fire department.

- Inform babysitters and caregivers of your plan.

© GREAT SOURCE. COPYING IS PROHIBITED.

ELIMINATE HAZARDS, INCLUDING...

- Bolting bookcases, china cabinets, and other tall furniture to wall studs.
- Installing strong latches on cupboards.
- Strapping the water heater to wall studs.

PREPARE A DISASTER SUPPLIES KIT FOR HOME & CAR, INCLUDING...

- First aid kit and essential medications.
- Canned food and can opener.
- At least three gallons of water per person.
- Protective clothing, rainwear, and bedding or sleeping bags.
- Battery-powered radio, flashlight, and extra batteries.
- Special items for infant, elderly, or disabled family members.
- Written instructions for how to turn off gas, electricity, and water if authorities advise you to do so. (Remember, you'll need a professional to turn natural gas service back on.)
- Keeping essentials, such as a flashlight and sturdy shoes, by your bedside.

KNOW WHAT TO DO WHEN THE SHAKING BEGINS

- DROP, COVER, AND HOLD ON! Move only a few steps to a nearby safe place. Stay indoors until the shaking stops and you're sure it's safe to exit. Stay away from windows. In a high-rise building, expect the fire alarms and sprinklers to go off during a quake.
- If you are in bed, hold on and stay there, protecting your head with a pillow.
- If you are outdoors, find a clear spot away from buildings, trees, and power lines. Drop to the ground.
- If you are in a car, slow down and drive to a clear place (as described above). Stay in the car until the shaking stops.

IDENTIFY WHAT TO DO AFTER THE SHAKING STOPS

- Check yourself for injuries. Protect yourself from further danger by putting on long pants, a long-sleeved shirt, sturdy shoes, and work gloves.
- Check others for injuries. Give first aid for serious injuries.
- Look for and extinguish small fires. Eliminate fire hazards. Turn off the gas if you smell gas or think it's leaking. (Remember, only a professional should turn it back on.)
- Listen to the radio for instructions.
- Expect aftershocks. Each time you feel one, DROP, COVER, AND HOLD ON!
- Inspect your home for damage. Get everyone out if your home is unsafe.
- Use the telephone only to report life-threatening emergencies. ❖

© GREAT SOURCE. COPYING IS PROHIBITED.

✳ List what you think are the six most important tips for you and your family to be prepared for earthquakes in the area where you live. When you finish, compare lists with a partner and make any changes or additions to your list that result from your conversation.

1 _____   4 _____

2 _____   5 _____

3 _____   6 _____

✳ Now design a guidebook to teach your family about how to be prepared for an earthquake. You have four pages in which to provide useful guidance for your family. Title the guidebook and put a heading on each page.

Title:

_____	_____
Page 1	Page 2
_____	_____
Page 3	Page 4

Connect what you read to real-life situations.

© GREAT SOURCE. COPYING IS PROHIBITED.

Exploring Multiple Perspectives

Almost daily we hear news reports describing how air pollution and deforestation, the loss of forests due to excessive logging, are putting our environment at risk. Other stories tell about the depletion of natural resources such as water, oil, and healthy soil. Opinions vary about how we can best protect our natural resources. Some news reports provide facts about the issues. Other newspaper or magazine articles want to **persuade** you to accept certain viewpoints or engage in particular actions.

In this unit, you will read persuasive essays about environmental issues. As you read each article, you will learn more about the techniques of persuasion. You will also be asked to think about whether or not the authors are convincing. Which authors offer examples and evidence that persuade you to believe them, despite the **multiple perspectives** on environmental issues?

In addition to reading, you will apply techniques of persuasion to your own writing. You will try to convince others to consider your point of view about saving a particular natural resource.

© GREAT SOURCE. COPYING IS PROHIBITED.

51

PROBLEM AND SOLUTIONS

You've probably heard this question asked many times at the grocery store: Paper or plastic? Maybe you've heard it so often that you don't even think about it any more. In the following essay, the authors ask you to consider how much we rely on paper products. But we rely on plastic as well. Plastic bags line our trash cans. They keep our bread and vegetables fresh. We use them to hold our lunches. Is paper a better alternative than plastic? Are there other alternatives available?

As you read "Are Plastic Bags Harming the Environment?" focus on what the authors are trying to persuade you to believe. One technique writers use is to describe the **problem** clearly and to offer **solutions.** Ask yourself: What is the *problem* the authors identify and what *solutions* do they suggest?

Underline words and phrases that emphasize the problem the authors identify. Circle any solutions they offer. In your **Response Notes,** write questions or comments you have about the writers' viewpoints.

Response Notes

"Are Plastic Bags Harming the Environment?"
by John Roach and written by Sara Ives

"Paper or plastic?" Nearly every time someone buys groceries, he or she is asked this question. The answer is not as easy as it may seem. According to environmentalists, plastic bags and paper bags both have drawbacks.

Plastic bags are everywhere. According to the Virginia-based American Plastics Council, 80 percent of groceries are packed in plastic bags.

"The numbers are absolutely staggering," said Vincent Cobb, a business-person from Chicago who launched reusablebags.com. He notes that consumers use between 500 billion and 1 trillion plastic bags per year worldwide.

Plastic bags can be found in landfills, stuck on trees, and floating in the ocean.

What is the effect of all of these bags? Some experts say that they harm the environment. Plastic bags can take hundreds of years to break down. As they break down, they release poisonous materials into the water and soil.

Plastic bags in the ocean can choke and strangle wildlife. Endangered sea turtles eat the bags and often choke on them—probably because the bags look like jellyfish, the main food of many sea turtles.

In fact, floating plastic bags have been spotted as far north as the Arctic Ocean to as far south as the southern end of South America. One expert predicts that within ten years, plastic bags will wash up in Antarctica!

© GREAT SOURCE. COPYING IS PROHIBITED.

Despite these negative effects, plastic bags do have some advantages.

"Plastic grocery bags are some of the most reused items around the house," explained Laurie Kusek of the American Plastics Council.

Plastic bags hold school lunches, line trash cans, and serve as gym bags. These uses decrease plastic bag waste.

According to the Film and Bag Federation, a trade group within the Society of Plastics Industry, paper bags use more energy and create more waste than plastic bags.

Plastic bags require 40 percent less energy to produce than paper bags and cause 70 percent less air pollution, the group explained. Plus, plastic bags release as much as 94 percent less waste into the water.

Paper bags do, however, break down more quickly than plastic bags. They also don't strangle wildlife.

What, then, should people do?

While some experts have argued for placing a tax on plastic bags, others worry that the tax would cause people who make plastic bags to lose jobs. Some people also worry that making plastic bags more expensive (through taxes) would increase landfill waste because stores would start using paper bags again.

Another possible solution would be to use biodegradable plastic bags, a technology that has recently improved. "Biodegradable" means that the bags naturally break down, like, for example, a banana peel does when you leave it outside.

Perhaps the simplest solution for now, however, is to pack groceries in reusable bags, such as cloth tote bags. ❖

❊ Take a minute to list the types of paper products you use each day.

© GREAT SOURCE. COPYING IS PROHIBITED.

✳ On the chart below, list the problems the authors identify in "Are Plastic Bags Harming the Environment?" List the solutions they propose.

Problems Identified	Solutions Proposed

✳ Compare your chart with a partner's. Then write one paragraph in which you describe your reaction to this article. What is the authors' perspective on the use of plastic bags? What details reveal that perspective? Are you convinced?

_____

_____

_____

_____

_____

_____

_____

_____

_____

_____

_____

_____

_____

_____

Determine the problems posed. Look for the solutions offered to help you understand the author's perspective.

© GREAT SOURCE. COPYING IS PROHIBITED.

52 LESSON

Make a mental picture of the pile of paper you use in a week. Remember that it takes wood and electricity to produce even a simple sheet of paper or a roll of paper towels. Now imagine how much wood and electricity it takes to produce the paper you use each *year*. How could you reduce your paper usage? What other resource-saving habits might you develop?

One strategy a writer uses in **persuasive writing** is to provide convincing details to readers. In the following article, the authors present facts about the consumption of natural resources. As you read, keep track of which **details** are convincing to you and which details you question. Use your **Response Notes** to raise questions and make comments about the details the authors provide.

"Call of the Mall" from *You Are the Earth*
by David Suzuki and Kathy Vanderlinden

Response Notes

. . . It can be fun to buy a great new outfit or the latest CD. But is that the only thing that's fun or has any value? For many people, it seems that it is. Buying more and more objects is a major way people today look for happiness and purpose in life. Look at these facts:

- Toy makers produce up to 6000 new toys each year. (That's on top of the old toys already for sale).

- Americans spend an average of 6 hours a week shopping. They spend just 40 minutes a week playing with their children.

- We can choose from more than 11,000 magazines and 25,000 supermarket items, including 200 kinds of cereal.

- North Americans will spend an average of two years of their lives just watching TV commercials.

But owning things by itself doesn't seem to make people happy. Buying something makes you feel happy for a little while. Then you have to buy something else to feel happy again. Meanwhile, all this shopping is eating up the Earth. Many natural resources, such as oil, trees, and aluminum, are used to make, advertise, and sell all those things we buy. Added to that is the waste these purchases create—the bags and boxes they come in, the advertising flyers, and the things themselves when we throw them away. This mountain of garbage gets burned in incinerators, dumped into lakes, or buried in the ground, where it contaminates the air, water, and soil.

© GREAT SOURCE. COPYING IS PROHIBITED.

- In the last 60 years, Americans alone have used up as large a share of the Earth's mineral resources as all people in the world used before that time.
- In the last 200 years, the United States has lost 85 percent of its old-growth forests, 50 percent of its wetlands, and 99 percent of its tall grass prairies.

Get the connection? ❖

❋ How convincing are the authors? Chart your understanding below.

Problems Identified	Solutions Proposed	Convincing Details

❋ Now that you have read these authors' perspectives, consider how you would answer the question: paper or plastic? Write a note to your family to convince them to accept your viewpoint. Provide convincing details from your own experience or from those given by the authors to justify your perspective on the paper or plastic question.

Evaluate the details provided to help you understand the authors' opinions.

© GREAT SOURCE. COPYING IS PROHIBITED.

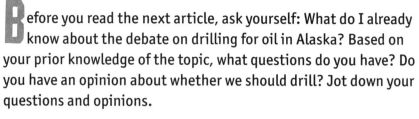

Before you read the next article, ask yourself: What do I already know about the debate on drilling for oil in Alaska? Based on your prior knowledge of the topic, what questions do you have? Do you have an opinion about whether we should drill? Jot down your questions and opinions.

_____

_____

_____

_____

Another strategy a writer might use in persuasive writing is to offer alternative positions for readers to think about. As you read the following article, highlight the alternatives the author points out about drilling for oil in Alaska. Make comments in the **Response Notes** about the perspectives offered.

Response Notes

"To Drill or Not to Drill" by Steven R. Wills

It is history class after lunch, and you are just falling to sleep. A large, fluffy hand reaches down and carries your history teacher away as she continues to describe the presidential election of 1868. Yes, you realize, this is a dream.

Suddenly you are behind the wheel of a massive SUV. You notice that you are running out of gas, and also notice a gas station just up ahead. You drive up to the pump, but find that a majestic Alaskan caribou is standing in your way. He's beautiful, but you need to fill up. It occurs to you that the only way you'll be able to get gas is to run him down.

The teacher shouts your name and you wake up, leaving a small puddle of drool on your desk.

Turns out your dream was also a metaphor—a visual symbol of the kinds of decisions lawmakers, oil companies, oil consumers, and environmental activists are facing today. "To drill or not to drill?!" *That* is the question.

At the heart of the problem is America's hunger for oil. The United States is, by far, the largest consumer of oil in the world—using more than 7,000,000,000 (yep, that's billion) barrels of oil each year. We use it to heat our homes and businesses, and to manufacture plastics, tires, ink, and synthetic fibers. And mostly, we use it to operate our cars, trucks, and other vehicles (almost five billion barrels each year).

© GREAT SOURCE. COPYING IS PROHIBITED.

Although we import most of our oil from other countries, we realize that dependence gives the oil-producing countries a certain power over us. We learned that lesson from the oil crisis of the 1970s, caused by a Middle East oil embargo by the OPEC (Oil Producing and Exporting Countries) organization.

However, large oil reserves have been found under the frozen tundra of Alaska, on land, which, in 1960, was set aside to be protected as the Arctic National Wildlife Refuge (ANWR). When parts of ANWR were opened up to drilling in the 1980s, what followed was pollution, truck and drilling noise, chemical waste pits, and the 1989 disastrous oil spill from the *Exxon Valdez*.

Today, more oil reserves have been located on the ANWR, and sides are lining up to either support or oppose drilling for more oil. The opposing arguments sound like this:

No Drilling! Haven't we learned our lesson? The ANWR is rich in wildlife. It is home to bears (grizzly and Kodiak—both endangered), wolves, foxes, musk oxen, millions of migratory birds, and caribou. The caribou are of particular concern, since they move over the very areas targeted for drilling in order to reach their traditional breeding grounds.

The environment will be altered for other reasons, as well. You can't just pull oil from the ground—you need drilling platforms, trucking roads, pipelines, and a constant supply of heavy equipment. When will we finally take a stand and say, "Remember the *Exxon Valdez*? Not again! This last piece of wilderness must be preserved!"

Drill Away! We now have the ability to limit environmental damage. Trucking roads in the winter can be made of crushed ice, and supplies can be flown in by helicopter in the summer. Furthermore, high-tech drilling techniques mean that fewer drilling platforms need to be built. New pipelines can be elevated five feet off the ground so that wildlife can easily pass under. Also, the pipes will not be fitted with flat valves (which can fail and leak), but rather with loops that will limit the spill from any possible leak. Finally, all waste will be recycled.

No Drilling! Ice roads solve problems but create others, since they would require millions of gallons of precious fresh water—water that would likely come from the same sources that serve the plants of the tundra. Also, while high-tech devices help, they cannot eliminate accidents or potential disasters. Besides, who says drilling companies will follow all of these high-tech guidelines?

Drill Away! The new oil reserves are estimated to contain from 3.7 to 16 billion barrels of oil. That's anywhere from a six-month to two-year supply. Not only will that oil help curb our dependence on imports, but it will also generate big bucks for the local towns and people.

No Drilling! Why not increase the fuel efficiency of vehicles? A minor increase in auto and truck fuel efficiency would save more oil than would be found in the Alaskan reserves. ❖

© GREAT SOURCE. COPYING IS PROHIBITED.

NO doubt this is a tough call, but a decision must be made about whether to drill on the ANWR. How would you face this problem?

✳ List the most persuasive details in the article for each of the positions in the debate. Share your list with a partner and discuss which alternative is most convincing to each of you and why.

Examining the Alternatives	
To Drill	Not to Drill

✳ Now that you have read about the debate, form an opinion about drilling in the Arctic National Wildlife Refuge. Write a paragraph explaining your opinion. Include details from the article that support your opinion.

_____
_____
_____
_____
_____
_____
_____
_____
_____
_____
_____
_____

Examine the alternative perspectives the author uses to persuade you to consider an important problem and its potential solutions.

© GREAT SOURCE. COPYING IS PROHIBITED.

MAKING CONNECTIONS TO OUR LIVES

Farmers have become increasingly dependent on chemicals that help crops grow faster, protect them from insects or other pests, and increase yields. At the same time, some scientists and environmentalists have warned of the dangers of overusing chemical treatments. There are farmers who maintain organic farms, but the methods are more expensive and labor intensive. How conscientious are your family and friends about buying organic products? Does an organic label necessarily mean the product is chemical free? How is the issue of chemicals in food related to the earlier lessons about protecting our natural resources?

Writers know that readers respond when they can **make connections.** When a writer connects one situation to something the reader is familiar with, the author can make a persuasive case. Jane Goodall, the woman who is famous for her work with chimpanzees, has taken up another cause in science—our awareness of how food production affects our health and environment. Her perspective as a scientist affects what she writes and how she writes it.

As you read this excerpt from Goodall's book on the use of pesticides, highlight and write reactions in your **Response Notes** to the connections you make between what she describes, what you know about the use of chemicals, and how you think the issue relates to you.

➤ from **Harvest for Hope: A Guide to Mindful Eating**
by Jane Goodall with Gary McAvoy and Gail Hudson

Response Notes

Growing Food with Poisons

Ever since World War II, when scientists first figured out that nerve gas used in warfare could be turned on crop-eating insects, the farm industry has become increasingly dependent on the chemical industry. And this has turned out to be an unholy—and a very destructive—alliance. Nature has bestowed all living things with the instinct to survive—adaptation to adversity is the key to evolutionary survival. When chemical pesticides are first introduced into an area, insect predators will quickly be poisoned and die. But gradually, after repeated applications, some insects will build up resistance. Just as overuse of antibiotics creates antibiotic-resistance in the bacteria that cause sicknesses in animals and human, heavy does of pesticides create pesticide-resistance in insects. After more than fifty years of farming with pesticides, there are whole populations of "pest" insects that have evolved to become

© GREAT SOURCE. COPYING IS PROHIBITED.

increasingly impervious to pesticides. The response of the farmer is to spray more often, and with increasingly more toxic pesticides. Nowadays, it's not uncommon for farmers to use three times as many chemicals as they needed forty years ago to kill off the same insects. It's the same situation with using chemicals to ward off marauding weeds, rodents, and diseases: Farmers are using more and more chemicals and finding them less and less effective. Each year, about three million tons of farm chemicals are applied to the surface of this planet.

And all these chemicals, of course, don't just stay on the farm: They escape into the environment. They evaporate into the jet stream and fall in our rain and snowflakes; they are lifted by the wind and drift into our back-yards, our playgrounds, our preserved wild lands, and even our organic farms; they sink into the soil and leach into our groundwater, reservoirs, and wells; they find their way into our lakes, rivers, and oceans; and, of course, they can end up in the bodies of animals and people.

What's the collateral damage caused by these chemical assassins? For one thing, it's estimated that only 0.1 percent of applied pesticides reach the target pests, meaning all kinds of innocent bystanders suffer. Sometimes the immune and reproductive systems of honeybees are so compromised by pesticide exposure that they can't produce honey. Agricultural chemicals, combined with industrial and domestic chemicals, that enter the rivers and oceans weaken the immune systems of dolphins, whales, and thousands of other aquatic creatures. They cause birth defects in frogs and other amphibians—such as hind legs that are fused together or extra legs sprouting from their bellies or backs. When orcas are washed up on the shores of British Columbia their bodies are so contaminated with PCBs that they are regarded as hazardous toxic waste. And their calves die from drinking their mothers' toxic milk.

Farm chemicals kill of as many as 67 million American birds each year. I heard the other day that the songbirds that once greeted the spring in Iowa with their joyous chorus have virtually gone from the farming areas. In other words, farming chemicals are destroying our wild flora and fauna. The prophecy of Rachel Carson, in her seminal book, *Silent Spring*, has been fulfilled in many other places.

© GREAT SOURCE. COPYING IS PROHIBITED.

✻ In the Double-Entry Log below, list the dangers Goodall discusses that made the strongest impression on you. In the right column, explain how you can connect these dangers to your life.

DOUBLE-ENTRY LOG

Goodall's example of dangers	*Connections to my life*

✻ Demonstrate how Goodall's discussion of chemical poisons is important to your life by using the space provided to write the beginning of a short story in which you are the main character. The story should focus on the effect of some chemical hazard on you, the main character.

_____

_____

_____

_____

_____

_____

_____

_____

_____

_____

_____

_____

_____

_____

Notice how the author makes connections to readers' lives to persuade them to be concerned about today's problems.

© GREAT SOURCE. COPYING IS PROHIBITED.

On average, each person in a developed country uses as much energy in six months as a citizen of a developing country such as Nepal uses in his or her lifetime.

As you read, underline the actions you are willing to take to reduce the amount of energy you consume. Underline, too, alternative ways to produce energy. In your **Response Notes,** list actions not included in the excerpt that you are willing to take to use less energy.

"Save Your Energy" from *You Are the Earth* by David Suzuki and Kathy Vanderlinden

Response Notes

What can we do? For a start, we can stop wasting energy. We can do this in simple ways, such as turning off lights when we aren't using them, lowering the thermostats in our homes at night, and using energy-efficient fluorescent lights whenever possible. We can also walk, skate, or bike more instead of riding in cars. It's a lot more fun to do these things, and it's good for our health and the Earth's health, too.

We can also make bigger changes as communities and nations. Instead of relying on fossil fuels, we can use energy sources that don't pollute and will never run out. For instance, in places near the ocean, the power of tides can drive turbines, which are wheel-like devices with blades that help them rotate. The turbines are connected to generators, which produce electricity. In windy regions, wind can also drive turbines to produce electricity. And best of all, the bountiful power of sunlight can be captured to heat and light homes, heat water, and generate electricity. Perhaps you have a calculator or a game that uses solar power. These sources of energy are being used in small ways today but show promise of having much wider uses in the future. ❖

© GREAT SOURCE. COPYING IS PROHIBITED.

✳ Make a list of things your school and your class can do to help solve some of the energy consumption problems we face today.

_____

_____

_____

_____

Compare your list with that of a partner. Add anything to your list that comes to mind after your discussion with your partner.

✳ Using what you have learned in this unit about persuasive writing and about environmental concerns, write a persuasive letter to your principal asking him or her to support a school-wide project to promote awareness of and to take action against unnecessary consumption of energy.

_____

_____

_____

_____

_____

_____

_____

_____

_____

_____

_____

_____

Analyze techniques of persuasion and use them in your own writing to convince your reader to consider your viewpoints.

_____

_____

© GREAT SOURCE. COPYING IS PROHIBITED.

Focusing on Language and Craft

We live in a world of symbols. Our reality is made up of things—animals, plants, people, cars, houses, electronics, and so on. As soon as we begin to see a meaning beyond these things, however, we move into the world of symbols. When a car becomes not only a means of transportation but a mark of how much money one has, it is a symbol.

There are symbols that are recognized only by certain groups of people. Think about sports teams and their symbols, your school and its colors or mascot, certain kinds of cars, and music groups.

In this unit, you will look at **reading and writing** in somewhat unconventional ways. You'll see how you can "read the world"; and you'll look at how **symbols** were very much a part of primitive writing. Throughout the unit you'll focus on developing your understanding of **symbolism,** which is basic to language and craft.

© GREAT SOURCE. COPYING IS PROHIBITED.

What do you mean by the word *reading?* With your class-mates, come up with as many definitions or examples of reading as you can, and have someone post them on the board or on chart paper.

As you work, ask yourselves questions such as these:

- What does it mean for a child to learn to "read"?
- How is reading the words of a song different from reading a textbook?
- How is watching ads on television a kind of "reading"?
- What does it mean for a naturalist to "read" signs of animals in the woods?
- What does "reading" music mean?
- How is reading a novel like or different from reading a manual on setting up a new DVD player?

✳ Use this space for notes:

✳ When you have run out of answers, or you have run out of space to write, write your own definition of reading. Make it as imaginative as you can.

My definition of reading:

_____

_____

_____

Read Gwendolyn Brooks's poem about Martin Luther King, Jr., on page 179.

© GREAT SOURCE. COPYING IS PROHIBITED.

Martin Luther King Jr. by Gwendolyn Brooks

A man went forth with gifts.

He was a prose poem.
He was a tragic grace.
He was a warm music.

He tried to heal the vivid volcanoes.
His ashes are
reading the world.

His Dream still wishes to anoint
the barricades of faith and of control.

His word still burns the center of the sun,
above the thousands and the
hundred thousands.

The word was Justice. It was spoken.
So it shall be spoken.
So it shall be done.

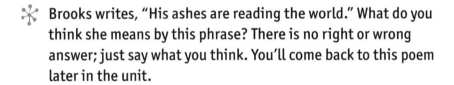

* Brooks writes, "His ashes are reading the world." What do you think she means by this phrase? There is no right or wrong answer; just say what you think. You'll come back to this poem later in the unit.

_____

_____

Alberto Manguel, in his book *A History of Reading,* writes that "reading letters on a page is only one of its many guises." He goes on to list many kinds of reading:

The astronomer reading a map of stars that no longer exist;
the Japanese architect reading the land on which a house is to be built so as
to guard it from evil forces;
the zoologist reading the spoor of animals in the forest;
the card-player reading her partner's gestures before playing the winning
card;
the dancer reading the choreographer's notations, and the public reading the
dancer's movements on the stage;
the weaver reading the intricate design of a carpet being woven;

© GREAT SOURCE. COPYING IS PROHIBITED.

Response Notes

the organ-player reading various simultaneous strands of music orchestrated
   on the page;
the parent reading the baby's face for signs of joy or fright or wonder;
the Chinese fortune-teller reading the ancient marks on the shell of a
   tortoise; . . .
the psychiatrist helping patients read their own bewildering dreams;
the Hawaiian fisherman reading the ocean currents by plunging a hand into
   the water;
the farmer reading the weather in the sky—
all these share with book-readers the craft of deciphering and translating
   signs. ❖

✳ **Pick three of Manguel's examples of "reading" and draw the
images they represent to you. In the top row of the chart below,
write Manguel's words for the images you are sketching.**

Example 1	Example 2	Example 3

© GREAT SOURCE. COPYING IS PROHIBITED.

Manguel says "We all read ourselves and the world around us in order to glimpse what and where we are. We read to understand, or to begin to understand."

❋ Use this quotation as the beginning of a brief essay in which you explain what kinds of reading are important to you. Be as specific as you can as you elaborate on your ideas.

_____
_____
_____
_____
_____
_____
_____
_____
_____
_____
_____
_____
_____
_____
_____
_____
_____
_____
_____
_____
_____
_____
_____

Reading has a much broader
meaning than simply deciphering
text on a page.

© GREAT SOURCE. COPYING IS PROHIBITED.

Most of us take writing for granted. We go to school, we learn to read and we learn to write. We don't question the existence of writing. It's strange to think that at one time, there was no such thing as writing.

Here is part of an essay that explains Don Lago's idea of how writing started. Read it, first without using the **Response Notes** column.

Symbols of Humankind by Don Lago

Response Notes

Many thousands of years ago, a man quietly resting on a log reached down and picked up a stick and with it began scratching upon the sand at his feet. He moved the stick slowly back and forth and up and down, carefully guiding it through curves and straight lines. He gazed upon what he had made, and a gentle satisfaction lighted his face.

Other people noticed this man drawing on the sand. They gazed upon the figures he had made, and though they at once recognized the shapes of familiar things such as fish or birds or humans, they took a bit longer to realize what the man had meant to say by arranging these familiar shapes in this particular way. Understanding what he had done, they nodded or smiled in recognition.

This small band of humans didn't realize what they were beginning. The images these people left in the sand would soon be swept away by the wind, but their new idea would slowly grow until it had remade the human species. These people had discovered writing.

Writing, early people would learn, could contain much more information than human memory could and contain it more accurately. It could carry thoughts much farther than mere sounds could—farther in distance and in time. Profound thoughts born in a single mind could spread and endure.

The first written messages were simply pictures relating familiar objects in some meaningful way—pictographs. Yet there were no images for much that was important in human life. What, for instance, was the image for sorrow or bravery? So from pictographs humans developed ideograms to represent more abstract ideas. An eye flowing with tears could represent sorrow, and a man with the head of a lion might be bravery. ❖

✳ Now reread the first part of the essay. This time, beside each paragraph, use the **Response Notes** column to make a simple drawing (like a pictograph) that relates to the text.

© GREAT SOURCE. COPYING IS PROHIBITED.

✳ Compare your drawings with those of your partner or your group.

- How similar are they?
- How do they differ?
- Can you tell from the drawings what the paragraph is about?

In the essay, Don Lago writes about the origin of *ideograms,* pictures that represent abstractions rather than concrete objects. He wrote, "Yet there were no images for much that was important in human life. What, for instance, was the image for sorrow or bravery? So from pictographs humans developed ideograms to represent more abstract ideas. An eye flowing with tears could represent sorrow, and a man with the head of a lion might be bravery."

✳ With your partner or group, make a list of some other abstract ideas that are as important in human life as sorrow and bravery.

✳ Write at least three items from your list here. For each one, design an *ideogram* that could represent that concept.

Abstract idea	Ideogram for the abstract idea

✳ Notice that this essay is titled "Symbols of Humankind." After reading the first part of the essay and working with the concept of ideograms, what do you think would be a good definition of the word *symbol*? Write your ideas here, then compare your definition with the definitions of your group.

_____

_____

_____

_____

_____

Ideas can be expressed through pictures and words.

© GREAT SOURCE. COPYING IS PROHIBITED.

The story of "Symbols of Humankind" continues in Don Lago's essay. Read this final part of the essay, using your **Response Notes** column in the usual way. Make notes, ask questions, notice any ideas new to you, and make connections to what you already know or have experienced.

Response Notes

Symbols of Humankind by Don Lago *(continued)*

The next leap occurred when the figures became independent of things or ideas and came to stand for spoken sounds. Written figures were free to lose all resemblance to actual objects. Some societies developed syllabic systems of writing in which several hundred signs corresponded to several hundred spoken sounds. Others discovered the much simpler alphabetic system, in which a handful of signs represented the basic sounds the human voice can make.

At first, ideas flowed only slightly faster when written than they had through speech. But as technologies evolved, humans embodied their thoughts in new ways: through the printing press, in Morse code, in electromagnetic waves bouncing through the atmosphere and in the binary language of computers.

Today, when the Earth is covered with a swarming interchange of ideas, we are even trying to send our thoughts beyond our planet to other minds in the Universe. Our first efforts at sending our thoughts beyond Earth have taken a very ancient form: pictographs. The first message, on plaques aboard Pioneer spacecraft launched in 1972 and 1973, featured a simple line drawing of two humans, one male and one female, the male holding up his hand in greeting. Behind them was an outline of the Pioneer spacecraft, from which the size of the humans could be judged. The plaque also included the "address" of the two human figures: a picture of the solar system, with a spacecraft emerging from the third planet. Most exobiologists believe that when other civilizations attempt to communicate with us they too will use pictures.

All the accomplishments since humans first scribbled in the sand have led us back to where we began. Written language only works when two individuals know what the symbols mean. We can only return to the simplest form of symbol available and work from there. In interstellar communication, we are at the same stage our ancestors were when they used sticks to trace a few simple images in the sand.

We still hold their sticks in our hands and draw pictures with them. But the stick is no longer made of wood; over the ages that piece of wood has been transformed into a massive radio telescope. And we no longer scratch on sand; now we write our thoughts onto the emptiness of space itself. ❖

© GREAT SOURCE. COPYING IS PROHIBITED.

✳ Choose one of the following quotations taken from the second part of Don Lago's essay and expand on it. Use the quotation as a starting point to explore your own ideas about what Lago says. Use specific incidents or examples from your own experience.

1. "All the accomplishments since humans first scribbled in the sand have led us back to where we began."

2. "Written language only works when two individuals know what the symbols mean."

3. "And we no longer scratch on sand; now we write our thoughts onto the emptiness of space itself."

Writing has evolved from simple pictographs to symbols conveying our deepest thoughts.

© GREAT SOURCE. COPYING IS PROHIBITED.

In this unit you have looked at reading and writing in somewhat unconventional ways. You have looked at *reading* as a way of making meaning from many aspects of our universe, rather than just making meaning from texts on a page. You have read that *writing* is made up of the symbols we use to represent both things and ideas.

In this lesson you're going to write a series of simple statements that will become a poem illustrating the definitions of *image, simile, metaphor,* and *symbol.*

STEP ONE: THE IMAGE

Definition: An image describes how something looks, sounds, feels, smells, or tastes. It presents a specific sensory description.

Choose something, such as an animal, plant, or object that you can describe. Write a simple sentence about your subject.

Example: The *heron* stands tall, unblinking in the early morning sun.

Write a sentence that describes the subject, or the image, you have chosen:

_____

_____

_____

STEP TWO: THE SIMILE

Definition: A simile is a stated comparison. It compares one thing with another using the words "like" or "as."

Use the subject you described and write a simile using "like" or "as."

Example: The heron *is like* a mysterious stranger, barely visible through the mist.

Write a sentence that compares your subject to something else (simile):

_____

_____

_____

© GREAT SOURCE. COPYING IS PROHIBITED.

STEP THREE: THE METAPHOR

Definition: A metaphor is an implied comparison. It speaks of one thing in terms of another.

Look again at the poem about Martin Luther King, Jr., in Lesson 51 and find these lines that are all metaphors:

> He was a prose poem.
> He was a tragic grace.
> He was a warm music.

Notice how Gwendolyn Brooks uses them to build her impressions of King.

✳ Write another comparison for your subject, but don't use "like" or "as."

Example: On the ground, it is a shadow of itself, emerging and fading in the swirling fog.

Write a sentence with another comparison without using "like" or "as" (metaphor):

_____

_____

_____

_____

STEP FOUR: THE SYMBOL

Definition: A symbol means both what it is and something else. It stands for something beyond the concrete image.

✳ Write one more simple sentence about your subject. This time be aware of all that you have already written.

Example: The heron shifts, rises on unfolding wings—*the stranger floats away.*

Write a last sentence describing something your subject does; try to take the image to a new level so that it becomes a symbol.

_____

_____

_____

_____

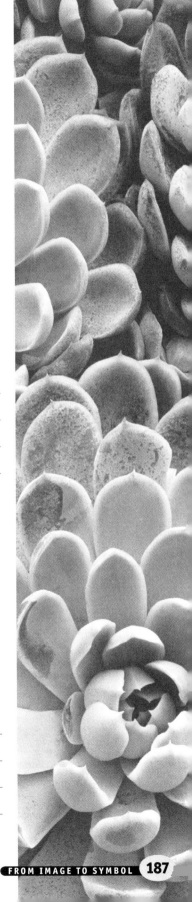

© GREAT SOURCE. COPYING IS PROHIBITED.

STEP FIVE: PUTTING IT ALL TOGETHER

❋ Give your poem a title that conveys the idea of
the evolving symbol. Below is an example of the
finished poem illustrating image, simile, metaphor,
and symbol.

The Radiant Bird

Image:
The heron stands tall,
unblinking in the early morning
sun

Simile:
The heron is like a
mysterious stranger, barely
visible through the mist.

Metaphor:
On the ground, it is a shadow of
itself, emerging and fading
in the swirling fog.

Symbol:
The heron shifts, rises
on unfolding wings—
the stranger floats away.

© GREAT SOURCE. COPYING IS PROHIBITED.

Write your finished poem here. Don't forget the title!

_____

_____

_____

_____

_____

_____

_____

_____

_____

_____

_____

_____

_____

_____

_____

_____

_____

WORKING WITH YOUR GROUP

■ Share your poem with your group. Ask students to explain their
images, similes, metaphors, and *symbols.* For the symbol, try to
explain how the description of your subject in that stanza depends
for its meaning on all the previous stanzas.

■ Make any changes you think will improve your poem.

PRESENTATION

■ Write your poem on a piece of unlined paper, making the writing
resemble a type font that you like. Or type your poem on a
computer, and print it out using a very large font.

■ Illustrate your poem with drawings of the subject of your
poem. You might make just one drawing of your
subject or you might make one for each stanza.

Imagery, simile, metaphor,
and symbolism are tools
of the poet.

© GREAT SOURCE. COPYING IS PROHIBITED.

"The Road Not Taken," one of Robert Frost's best-known and best-loved poems, speaks to all of us. Who hasn't had difficulty making a decision at some point? Read and listen to this poem, first without making any notations.

The Road Not Taken by Robert Frost

Two roads diverged in a yellow wood,
And sorry I could not travel both
And be one traveler, long I stood
And looked down one as far as I could
To where it bent in the undergrowth;

Then took the other, as just as fair,
And having perhaps the better claim,
Because it was grassy and wanted wear;
Though as for that the passing there
Had worn them really about the same,

And both that morning equally lay
In leaves no step had trodden black.
Oh, I kept the first for another day!
Yet knowing how way leads on to way,
I doubted if I should ever come back.

I shall be telling this with a sigh
Somewhere ages and ages hence:
Two roads diverged in a wood, and I—
I took the one less traveled by,
And that has made all the difference. ❖

Response Notes

✻ Reread the poem, this time paying closer attention to how the narrator describes the two roads. First, circle words and lines that tell about the first road. Then underline words and phrases that tell about the second road. Finally, use the **Response Notes** column to record your questions, connections, and thoughts about the meaning of the poem.

© GREAT SOURCE. COPYING IS PROHIBITED.

✳ You have been working with the idea of *symbol* in poetry. What word in this poem is a symbol? Remember that to be a symbol, a word must stand both for itself and something beyond its literal meaning.

The symbol is _____.

It means _____.

In a few sentences, tell what this poem means to you.

_____

_____

_____

_____

Talk with your partner or group about the meaning of this poem. Share some stories about choices you have made when you had to decide which of two "roads" to take. The discussion will be preparation for writing your own symbolic poem.

PREWRITING Think about a choice you made in your life when you really had two options. The choice had consequences. State both options:

Option 1: _____

Option 2: _____

✳ Tell which option you took and what difference it has made in your life.

_____

_____

_____

_____

✳ Explain how you now feel about your choice. How has it changed your life? (Remember, Frost said his choice "made all the difference," but he doesn't tell us what that difference was.)

_____

_____

_____

_____

© GREAT SOURCE. COPYING IS PROHIBITED.

WRITING THE SYMBOLIC POEM Think of a symbol that can stand for the choice you had to make. Frost chose "two roads." Think of something that has meaning in its own right, such as *morning,* but also has a larger, symbolic meaning, such as, perhaps, *a beginning.*

Use the symbol you have chosen to tell about your choice. In your poem, tell

- what the choices were
- which choice you made
- what difference your decision has made in your life
- how you feel about that choice now

You may wish to use the form of Frost's poem as a model. When you finish, share your poem with your classmates.

Writing a symbolic poem helps you understand the meaning of literary symbols.

© GREAT SOURCE. COPYING IS PROHIBITED.

Studying
an Author

Reading several works by a single author helps you concentrate on the craft of writing, giving you ideas for different types of stories you can write.

Will Hobbs draws from his life experience, from research he has done, and from people he has known. He loves to hike, go whitewater rafting, and write books. As of 2005, he had written fifteen novels and two picture books. Many of his novels have won numerous awards. But he does not write for awards; he writes for his readers. He says, "My first hope for my novels is that they tell a good story, that the reader will keep turning the pages and will hate to see the story end. Beyond that, I hope to be inspiring a love for the natural world. I'd like my readers to appreciate and to care more about what's happening to wild creatures, wild places, and the diversity of life."

© GREAT SOURCE. COPYING IS PROHIBITED.

61 STORIES FROM OTHER STORIES

Where do writers get their ideas? Often they adapt a story, creating new characters in a new setting, but using the old story as a base. Science fiction and fantasy writers, for example, sometimes create their stories from myths and legends. They change the original stories to fit their purposes and to give the old stories new meanings. Will Hobbs says that he wanted to write because "I loved reading. If you like reading stories, you too might start thinking, I want to try that. I want to write a story." Some of Hobbs's novels are clearly connected to stories he has read.

In *The Maze,* Rick Walker is a troubled 14-year-old. Until he was 10, his grandmother raised him. When she died, he was placed in a series of foster homes. As the novel opens, he is sent to Blue Canyon Youth Detention Center for a minor offense. There, he spends a lot of time in the library, where Mr. B. befriends him and recommends books. As you read the excerpt, jot down in the **Response Notes** any questions or reactions you have.

from **The Maze** by Will Hobbs

Response Notes

Rick realized he'd gone on longer than usual with his reading warm-up. He turned to "Escape from the Maze" and read from the point where the greatest inventor of all time, Daedalus, was fashioning wings for himself and his son, Icarus, so they could fly out of the elaborate puzzle they were imprisoned in.

The wings worked all too well. Once they'd left their island prison behind, Icarus became intoxicated with the sensation of flight and started outflying the birds.

Suddenly Rick recalled that he'd heard this story before. His grandmother had read him a version of it when he was little.

He knew all about the intoxication of flight from way back, from a dream that had come almost nightly. In the dream he always had a miraculous, inexplicable power inside himself: he could actually fly. In the dream all he had to do was spread his arms and he'd begin to levitate higher and higher until he was hovering above the earth. Then he was not only hovering but actually flying above the fields and the treetops and the towns, weightless and peaceful and free.

Dream-flying had been his own great escape—he'd figured that out—a childish fantasy that had been gradually dying over the years and was nearly dead. He couldn't remember having had the flying dream a single time at Blue Canyon.

Rick remembered how Icarus' escape was going to end but he kept reading anyway. Ignoring his father's calls from below, Icarus flew higher and higher

© GREAT SOURCE. COPYING IS PROHIBITED.

until the sun melted the wax holding the invention together, and the boy fell into the sea.

Now Rick realized why he found the story of Icarus so appealing. His own life was a puzzle riddled with dead ends. His own life was a maze.

"From the expression on your face," Mr. B. said from his desk, "you're enjoying that book."

Almost always they talked about what Rick was reading. "Yeah," he said, "I kind of like it."

"So, what do you think of Greek mythology?"

"I can relate to it."

"How so?"

"Things just happen to people for no good reason. Because some god or other gets ticked at them."

"That's the way the ancient Greeks looked at the world, Rick, but we're not ancient Greeks. Americans believe you make your own luck, you know."

Rick didn't really believe it.... "I suppose."

"Hang in there, Rick. Your break will come. And when it does, you have to be willing to go for it. To see your break for what it is and dare to ride it with all that you've got." ❖

✳ **Write two things you know about Rick from this excerpt. What is he like?**

_____

_____

Rick runs away from the correctional facility when he learns that other inmates plan to beat him up for reporting that a guard was taking bribes. He ends up in The Maze, a labyrinth of canyons and rock formations in Canyonlands National Park in Utah. There he meets Lon Peregrino, an avid hang glider, who is releasing six condors into the wild in an attempt to restore the population of this endangered species. Rick is entranced by the beauty of the condors' flight, especially one he names Maverick who dares to fly higher and farther than the others. Yet, Lon is worried about Maverick's flying too close to the sun. Rick asks him about it.

"Isn't that what happened to Icarus, in the story from Greek mythology?"

"You know about Icarus! I love that story. But I have this theory, Rick.... I never bought the bit about the sun melting the wax that held the wings together. Everybody knows that as you go higher up in the atmosphere, it gets colder, not warmer."

© GREAT SOURCE. COPYING IS PROHIBITED.

"It's just a story, Lon."

"What if it *wasn't?* The Greeks were about the smartest people who ever lived, and Daedalus was the most brilliant inventor who ever lived. His time might have been thousands of years ago, but let's give him the credit he's due. Suppose for a minute that the Icarus story is a poetic account of something that *actually happened.*"

"That would be amazing."

"Imagine for a moment that Daedalus actually built two devices, very much like modern hang gliders, one for himself and one for his son."

"I like this theory of yours."

"Here's what happened. Very simply, Icarus got caught in a thermal he wasn't experienced enough to handle. It took him up and up, who knows how many thousands of feet up—"

"And then he tucked and tumbled into the sea."

"That's it."

"Icarus flew out of a maze, you know." ❖

❊ On the surface, this selection is about Icarus and Maverick, but on a deeper level it may be a story about Rick. Talk with a partner about the connections you see among the mythological characters of Daedalus and Icarus and the present-day fictional characters, Rick and Lon. Write your connections in the **Response Notes.**

❊ Rick cannot stay in Canyonlands forever. He will need to find his way out of that maze. Write a possible continuation of the story, based on what you have read and the connections you have made.

_____

_____

_____

_____

_____

_____

_____

_____

_____

_____

Giving a familiar story new twists allows the author to add layers of meaning.

© GREAT SOURCE. COPYING IS PROHIBITED.

Will Hobbs says, "About half of my ideas for stories come from my own life experiences, and the other half come from reading, as I learn more about whatever has sparked my interest." Life experience and research are obvious in all of Hobbs's novels.

Although Hobbs hiked all around The Maze in Canyonlands National Park, he did not hang glide. The life experiences he used for the hang gliding scenes included reading, imagining, and observing three hang glider pilots.

This excerpt begins after a rough launch, as Rick leaves the cliffs where he picked up the wind. As you read about Rick's flight to rescue Lon, made more dangerous because a storm is developing, think about how Hobbs puts you in the scene and increases suspense. Circle any words or phrases that make you feel as if you are there. Underline words or phrases that make the scene suspenseful. Write comments in the **Response Notes** about anything else that catches your attention.

from **The Maze** by Will Hobbs

Response Notes

After five rising revolutions he was satisfied that he was high enough above the cliffs to glide away from them and head for Jasper Canyon.

You're still alive, he told himself as he broke to the east and began to soar toward the Standing Rocks. A powerful wave of exhilaration washed over him. He suddenly realized he was whooping and shouting like a wild man, grinning from ear to ear. "Yes!" he was screaming. "Yes!"

On his left and below, a very large bird was flying in his direction. As it neared he saw the broad wings, the distinctive wing tips, the featherless gray head. Lon's missing condor, he realized. It was M1, returning home in advance of the storm.

A glance at the variometer told him he had risen from 6,200 feet at launch to 7,560. Concentrate, he told himself. Stay focused. Take a deep breath. This is just the beginning.

Over the Standing Rocks the glider took a powerful buffeting. He clung tight as the wing shuddered with the turbulence. The variometer kept chirping as the glider was rocked by more and more turbulence. Still, he pushed back slightly from the bar and kept rising. He needed altitude. It was taking all his strength to hang on to the control bar and fly the glider. He knew now for certain that he was inside a thermal, a very powerful thermal.

Rick saw the earth's spinning, dizzying retreat below him, and he fought the panic that accompanied his sudden loss of equilibrium.

© GREAT SOURCE. COPYING IS PROHIBITED.

Keep fighting, he told himself. Keep flying it. Don't let it get away from you.

He didn't know if he was strong enough to keep the wing tips down. One or the other kept threatening to go too high on him. He kept yanking hard on the side he wanted to bring down.

Ride it! Fight it!

Up, up, up he went, on an increasingly powerful column of rising air. He checked the variometer. He was at eleven thousand feet and climbing at a rate of a thousand feet per minute.

Eleven thousand feet!

It was getting cold. His face was cold, his teeth were cold.

High enough! There was a river below, but he couldn't tell which one. It was all a sickening blur.

He had to break out, find Jasper Canyon.

Rick pulled his weight over the bar, but the variometer kept chirping. A glance told him he was rising now at a rate of eighteen hundred feet per minute.

The turbulence was getting worse, much worse.

Ride it! Fight it!

• • •

Twelve thousand, thirteen thousand, fourteen thousand feet. It was becoming nearly impossible to hang on to the bar and keep the wings down. He didn't know how much longer he could hang on. He had to start thinking about the parachute.

Icarus, he thought ruefully. I'm pulling an Icarus. "Wasn't ready to fly a thermal," Lon had said.

Sixteen thousand feet. It was cold, cold, and getting harder to breathe.

From the variometer he glanced up and saw the base of a massive cumulus cloud not so far above. He could picture exactly what was going to happen, and soon. He was going to be inside that cloud and unable to tell up from down. Tucking and tumbling.

This is the way I'm going to die.

Wildly he forced his body as far forward of the control bar as he possibly could. He spread his hands wide and held on with all his strength.

Finally, finally, the glider nosed down. He heard the buzzing that told him he was losing altitude.

He kept his body forward of the bar, kept fighting the glider down. It felt like he was dropping fast, fast.

Suddenly the nose dived much more steeply than he wanted it to, and his stomach went into free fall. He pushed his body back, but not too far back. More than anything he didn't want to stall the glider.

Abruptly he found himself in relatively stable air, and realized what had happened. He'd just gone over the falls, and was free of the thermal. ❖

© GREAT SOURCE. COPYING IS PROHIBITED.

✳ Did you feel as if you were flying with Rick? Or could you imagine watching him soar above you? If so, that is because Hobbs used certain techniques to convey an experience in words. He used specific names of places. He focused on sensory details, and he used strong verbs to tell what was happening. With a partner, complete the first two columns of the following technique chart. Leave the third column blank for now.

TECHNIQUES USED TO CREATE AN EXPERIENCE IN WORDS

Technique	Hobbs's Examples	My Examples
Use specific names, places, and things	Jasper Canyon	
Focus on sensory details (how the experience sounded, looked, felt, and so on)	whooping and shouting	
Use strong verbs	fight, force	

✳ Now it's your turn. Plan and draft an Experience Snapshot. Think about an experience that you know well enough to recreate for a reader. Don't just describe it; use some of the techniques that Will Hobbs used to create an experience. Your experience can be one you actually had or one you have read about or imagined. Once you have an experience in mind, fill in the third column of the chart to help you plan what you will write. In the space below, write a draft of your Experience Snapshot.

_____

_____

_____

_____

_____

_____

_____

Writers recreate experiences for the reader by providing specific names and places, focusing on sensory details, and using strong verbs.

© GREAT SOURCE. COPYING IS PROHIBITED.

63 STORIES IN DIFFERENT GENRES

Will Hobbs likes to try new things, including finding different ways to tell stories. He has written fantasy, adventure, historical fiction, and mystery novels. How does he know which genre to use? The story suggests the **genre.** For example, he told an interviewer that when he wrote *Jason's Gold* he wanted "the sort of realism that could only be achieved by basing incidents in the novel on actual incidents from the Klondike gold rush." Hobbs included historical characters in the novel, such as the writer Jack London and the con man Soapy Smith.

Jason's Gold features 15-year-old Jason Hawthorn, who travels from New York to Seattle in 1897, planning to meet his brothers and beat other prospectors to the Klondike gold fields. When he arrives, his brothers have already left. Jason heads to the Yukon on his own, determined to find his brothers and his fortune.

Life is harsh for the prospectors who are unprepared for the rugged terrain and deep cold of the Yukon. Jason is smart and resourceful, and he gets some good breaks with help from Jack London and others he meets on the trail. But not everyone is so fortunate, as Jason discovers when he and his husky King hunt for the moose that will keep them alive. What they find is based on a true story. Note in the **Response Notes** any of Hobbs's writing techniques that you recognize from the last lesson. Remember, also, to note your questions and reactions.

from **Jason's Gold** by Will Hobbs

Response Notes

It was a gray day, threatening snow. It had warmed up to twenty below or even ten, he guessed. He was in despair of ever overtaking the two moose. As he turned another in the endless bends along the frozen river, he stopped dead in his tracks. He realized he'd lost the will to continue.

Something up ahead, it seemed, didn't quite fit the landscape—a crude log cabin at the edge of a clearing and slightly above the river.

Another mirage.

But the mirage wasn't going away. Maybe there *was* a cabin there.

He trudged closer. Yes, it really was a cabin, an extremely small one. His heart leaped, but then he realized there was no smoke coming from it. Never mind, they could be away hunting.

Look inside this cabin, then turn back around.

Up close, he was stunned to see a beaten trail leading from the cabin to the river, and the unmistakable tracks of snowshoes. There really *was* someone here!

© GREAT SOURCE. COPYING IS PROHIBITED.

"Hello?" he cried. "Is anybody in there?"

There were no windows to peek through. A piece of heavy tarp served for the door.

As his mitten pushed the canvas to one side, light fell on two bearded men in fur coats and fur hats. Startled, Jason jumped back, lost his grip on the tarp. "Ho in there!" he cried out—no reply. Once again he pushed the tarp aside. The bearded men were sitting on rounds of wood, right there, right there in front of him.

A cooking pot was suspended over a fire, but the fire had gone out.

The men weren't moving, he realized, and in the next instant he saw why. They were frozen solid.

He cried out in terror, then clamped his mouth shut. If the moose were close by, he'd spooked them.

He dropped the canvas over the opening and retreated. He stood there frozen by fright, with the husky puzzling at him. All he could think about was that this was how *he* was going to end up, and Charlie too.

He had to get one of those moose.

Wait, there might be some way to identify these two. Their kin would want to know.

He crawled back inside with the two men sitting by the dead fire. There was a piece of shoe leather sticking out of the ice in the bottom of their cooking pot. This was what starvation looked like.

Here, on the log wall, was what he was looking for—a message scrawled in pencil and punched over a nail:

> *Ours is the folly. Left Fort Simpson on the Mackenzie River.*
> *Seeking Dawson but lost. Too far, too late. Skin boat crushed*
> *by ice. Seen no game in weeks. Lack strength to continue.*
> > *God bless,*
> > *Samuel Whittaker and Villy Champlain*
> > *November, 30, 1897*

They'd written this message less than two weeks before. They had died, maybe, only days ago. Where was Fort Simpson? Where was the Mackenzie River?

Jason folded the paper and put it in the pocket of his coat, then secured the tarp over the door to keep the scavengers out. He started upstream, more desperate than ever to catch up with those moose. But then it started snowing, and heavily. Before long, all trace of their tracks was obliterated. ❖

Jason's Gold is **historical fiction** set in a specific time and place in history, the 1897 Klondike Gold Rush. It uses actual details to add realism to the fictional story. Jason Hawthorn did not exist, but many like him did.

© GREAT SOURCE. COPYING IS PROHIBITED.

✳ How has Hobbs recreated the experience for you? Explain in a short paragraph the techniques he used to weave history into an adventure story.

_____

_____

_____

_____

_____

Will Hobbs has also written **fantasy,** a genre characterized by talking animals and magical events. Hobbs wanted to write a novel that incorporated a magical flute and the legendary character Kokopelli, who was important to the ancient people of the Americas for his life-giving seeds. Hobbs, therefore, had to use elements of fantasy in *Kokopelli's Flute.*

Tepary Jones (Tep) finds a small stone flute in an ancient cave near his home in New Mexico. Although drawn to the flute, he waits until he is in his room that night to try it out. His only companion is his pet ringtail, Ringo, an animal like a raccoon who is an excellent hunter of mice. Read this once, just to get a sense of the story.

from **Kokopelli's Flute** by Will Hobbs

I turned my attention from Ringo to the ancient flute in my hands. It was only about four and a half inches long, so smooth, so ancient. . . . I was about to put the flute to my mouth when Ringo swooped down and knocked it free. The ringtail grabbed for it, but I'd already snatched it up. He sprang to my desktop a few feet away and started waving his tail like a battle flag.

I remember putting the flute to my lips and blowing on it a minute or two. The notes I was producing sounded as pure as falling water. I remember starting to feel dizzy . . . the room started spinning and reeling, and I was bucking like I was being ripped open and turned inside out. Next thing I knew, I had the sensation of having long black whiskers radiating out from my face. These whiskers almost hurt, they were so sensitive. My nose was twitching. I was aware of an alien scent, musky, overpowering, and close.

By now I was in a panic at whatever was happening, and Ringo was looking at me differently, strangely, starting to make those high-pitched ringtail hunting noises that sound like crackling static.

© GREAT SOURCE. COPYING IS PROHIBITED.

I didn't feel anything like myself, and when I looked at my hands, I could see why. I was looking at the five-clawed fingers of . . . a rat. I felt the bottom of my spine moving, and out of the corner of my eye I could see a long, bushy tail.

I jumped from the bed to the floor, but Ringo jumped just as quick. There was only a foot between us, and there was murder in his eye. "It's me!" I yelled at him. "It's Tep!" ❖

✳ Reread the excerpt. Mark the text where you find characteristics of the fantasy genre.

✳ Read the Experience Snapshot you drafted in Lesson 62. Outline the changes you would make in your writing if you were to rewrite it as fantasy or historical fiction or another genre you know well. Write or sketch a few notes for yourself in the space below.

✳ Rewrite your Experience Snapshot in a different genre, using your notes above.

Writers choose a genre to help them tell a story in a certain way. They select details for the story that fit that genre.

© GREAT SOURCE. COPYING IS PROHIBITED.

Compelling characters are essential to a good story. They do not need to be likeable, but they should be interesting. You wonder what will happen to them or how their actions will change the story. Developing **characters** can be hard work.

Will Hobbs told an interviewer, "For those kids in *Downriver,* I wrote pages and pages on each one before I ever started writing that story." *Downriver* tells the story of several teenagers with various problems. They have come together from all over the United States to an outdoor education school in Colorado, Discovery Unlimited. After experiencing whitewater rafting with Al, the leader, they decide that they can raft the Grand Canyon on their own, without a permit or expert leadership. They steal the rafts and van and leave Al behind—until he catches up with them far downriver. On the Colorado River, they learn whom to trust and whom to fear, and they learn about their own inner resources.

Sixteen-year-old Jessie narrates their story. The excerpt that follows is from the early part of their trip down the Grand Canyon, while they still feel confident about their ability and while they still have enough food for the trip. But then they hit a wild stretch of the river. Jessie and Troy are in one boat and the others are in the other boat. As you read, get a sense of who the characters are. Write your impressions and questions in the **Response Notes.**

from **Downriver** by Will Hobbs

Response Notes

We could hear another rapid coming, but we couldn't see it because it was on a sharp turn. "Should we scout it?" I asked Troy. He wagged his head. He was taken with the string of successes behind us, and having too much fun rowing to want to pull the boat to shore, tie it up, and go for a look. We rounded the bend in the center of the river and caught sight of a major hole only thirty or so feet in front of us.

There was no time to cock the boat and row to either side. All Troy could do was hit the hole straight on. I speared my weight to the very front as we dropped into the hole, and then I felt the oddest sensation. We had stopped moving. We were surfing in place. Suddenly the hole spun us sideways, and one side of the boat lifted up in the air as the low side was filling with water. My eyes met Troy's for a minute. He was at a loss. I lunged for the high side, to try to put some weight on it. Just as suddenly, the hole spit us out. "Bail!" Troy yelled. We were suddenly knee-deep in water.

© GREAT SOURCE. COPYING IS PROHIBITED.

Around the bend came the paddle raft, only they were on the inside of the turn as they approached the hole. They would have missed it, but they were paddling like crazy to line up for it on purpose. When they dropped into it, the hole spun them sideways too. They had no more control than a stick of driftwood. The black underside of their boat showed for a moment, and then the boat turned over. They'd flipped!

I saw swimmers. A couple of people were bobbing along in the river; Adam was hanging onto the chicken line on the overturned boat. Troy bent his back to the oars and towed toward an eddy, so we wouldn't be swept downstream. "Bail!" he yelled. "Boat's too heavy to row! Bail!"

I bailed like mad with that big bucket, and Troy caught the eddy. As the swimmers approached us, he rowed out into the current and I hauled Rita aboard. Troy intercepted Adam, who was clinging to the paddle raft. "We hit the hole straight on," Adam protested. "I don't know what happened."

Freddy and Pug, I could see, had reached the shore on their own, but where was Star?

"Over there!" I yelled, and pointed at Star in the river.

We dragged Star in. She was so weak, she couldn't help herself at all. She wasn't built with any insulation against that icy water, and as it turned out, she'd been held in the hole and given a thrashing.

We made a quick landfall, as Freddy and Pug ran downstream to join us. There was no beach there. It wasn't really a camp, but we had work to do, with the paddle raft to overturn, and little time—the sun was down from the canyon. We were all shivering, especially Star, whose eyes weren't even focusing. We had to get to the dry bags under the paddle raft, and put on some dry clothes. It took all of us, minus Star, to turn the boat over. Any kind of beach would've been handy, but there was a deep drop-off right at the bank. We had to use a lot of ropes, and pull on them with all our strength. For a while it looked like we wouldn't succeed. Three times the boat came about halfway up and then stalled. Adam said to Troy, "I sure hope that gear boat of yours never flips. It weighs about three times as much as this one."

We gave it one more try, and this time Pug went berserk, giving a ferocious battle cry and pulling on his rope like a Goliath. His mighty legs dug for traction, and in the end he fell into a pile of sharp rocks as the boat fell rightside up against the bank.

Pug came up full of scrapes and scratches, but he thought nothing of them, being the man of the moment and the recipient of truckloads of praise. He was beaming. That butch marine crewcut of his, about a month grown out, made him seem like a little fuzzball kid in a giant body, a little kid who only wanted the rest of the gang to like him. Rita went over to him and raised his right arm like a boxer's in triumph, then felt his biceps. "Hot stuff," she declared. ❖

© GREAT SOURCE. COPYING IS PROHIBITED.

✳ Discuss with a partner your impressions of the characters. Add other comments to your **Response Notes.**

When Hobbs told the interviewer that he had written pages and pages about the characters in *Downriver,* the interviewer asked if he wrote dialogue as well. Hobbs replied, "Both—the way they would talk, what they would wear, the kind of music they would listen to, the kind of friends they would have, what sorts of trouble they would have gotten into—just kind of jamming on ideas about everything on that kid."

✳ Choose one character who plays a role, or could play a role, in your Experience Snapshot from Lesson 62. For that character, jot down the kinds of descriptive details Hobbs wrote for his characters.

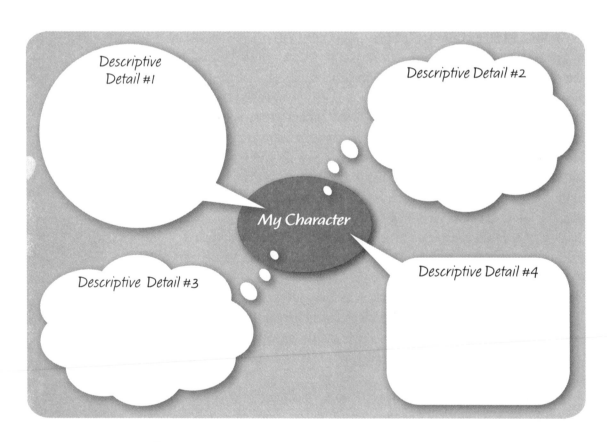

Descriptive Detail #1

Descriptive Detail #2

My Character

Descriptive Detail #3

Descriptive Detail #4

Authors need to know their characters well to make them come alive for the reader.

© GREAT SOURCE. COPYING IS PROHIBITED.

Will Hobbs wrote three complete drafts of *Downriver* before he felt that he had the narrator and the plot that he wanted. While he does not revise all of his books as extensively, he often stresses the importance of revision. In this lesson, you will use his advice to revise your Experience Snapshot.

Bearstone tells the story of Cloyd, a 14-year-old Native American boy sent to live in the mountains of Colorado with an old rancher. An early draft of the novel contains the following paragraph:

> He made a cut in the dozen or so peach trees, about a third of the way through. He didn't want them to die. He just wanted the leaves to wither and yellow, and the peaches to shrivel.

✳ **What do you know about Cloyd's feelings from this paragraph? What do you know about his motivation? Write your answers.**

_____

_____

_____

The published novel contains this paragraph:

> He cut through the skin of the nearest tree and winced as he withdrew the saw. Beads of moisture were forming along the edges of the fresh wound. From one to the next he ran with the saw roaring at full throttle, and he cut each of the twenty-two peach trees most of the way through. Each time, as the saw's teeth bit into the thick bark, he hollered with hurt as if he felt the saw himself. He didn't want to cut them down, he wanted them to die slowly. Before they died, their leaves would yellow and the peaches shrivel, and they would look just like his grandmother's peaches.

✳ **Now, what do you know about Cloyd's feelings and motivation? How does this paragraph make you feel? In the space below, write your answers to these questions.**

_____

_____

_____

© GREAT SOURCE. COPYING IS PROHIBITED.

The second paragraph is a revision. Will Hobbs explains, "Revision does not mean throwing out everything you have written and starting over. The part that I'd done well in the first version, I saved: 'their leaves would yellow and the peaches shrivel.' You learn to recognize what was good, and shouldn't be abandoned."

Review what you have drafted in this unit:

- a snapshot recreating an experience, real or imagined
- the same snapshot written in a different genre
- details about a character who plays a role in your Experience Snapshot

Decide what to keep and what to abandon. Revise one of your Experience Snapshots. You may want to use some of the techniques Will Hobbs used in the excerpts you read in this unit:

- putting a new twist on an old story
- providing specific names and places
- focusing on sensory details
- using strong verbs
- creating character sketches
- revising

✳ Write your revised snapshot here.

_____

_____

_____

_____

_____

_____

_____

_____

_____

_____

_____

_____

Writers can make their writing more effective by starting with a vision in the early drafts and continually refining the story through revisions.

© GREAT SOURCE. COPYING IS PROHIBITED.

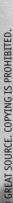
© GREAT SOURCE. COPYING IS PROHIBITED.

Assessing Your Strengths

You've reached the end of this *Daybook*. It's time to find out how you have grown as a reader and writer. The lessons in the *Daybook* have helped you develop skills and strategies to interact and connect with the stories and articles you read. You have considered multiple perspectives on a topic. You have looked carefully at language and craft. You have spent time focused on one particular author.

In this final unit, you will use these skills to read and respond to a story by well-known author Cynthia Rylant. Then you'll write your own story, using hers as your model. Finally, you'll **reflect on the progress** you've made toward your learning goals through this book.

As you read the first part of "Shells," pay attention to the conflict that exists between the characters. Try to imagine yourself in Michael's place. How would you feel? As you read, **interact** with the story by jotting down your first impressions and questions in the **Response Notes.**

Response Notes

"Shells" by Cynthia Rylant

"You hate living here."

Michael looked at the woman speaking to him.

"No, Aunt Esther. I don't." He said it dully, sliding his milk glass back and forth on the table. "I don't hate it here."

Esther removed the last pan from the dishwasher and hung it above the oven.

"You hate it here," she said, "and you hate me."

"I don't!" Michael yelled. "It's not you!"

The woman turned to face him in the kitchen.

"Don't yell at me!" she yelled. "I'll not have it in my home. I can't make you happy, Michael. You just refuse to be happy here. And you punish me every day for it."

"Punish you?" Michael gawked at her. "I don't punish you! I don't care about you! I don't care what you eat or how you dress or where you go or what you think. Can't you just leave me alone?"

He slammed down the glass, scraped his chair back from the table and ran out the door.

"Michael!" yelled Esther.

They had been living together, the two of them, for six months. Michael's parents had died and only Esther could take him in—or, only she had offered to. Michael's other relatives could not imagine dealing with a fourteen-year-old boy. They wanted peaceful lives.

Esther lived in a condominium in a wealthy section of Detroit. Most of the area's residents were older (like her) and afraid of the world they lived in (like her). They stayed indoors much of the time. They trusted few people. Esther liked living alone. She had never married or had children. She had never lived anywhere but Detroit. She liked her condominium.

But she was fiercely loyal to her family, and when her only sister had died, Esther insisted she be allowed to care for Michael. And Michael, afraid of going anywhere else, had accepted.

Oh, he was lonely. Even six months after their deaths, he still expected to see his parents—sitting on the couch as he walked into Esther's living room,

© GREAT SOURCE. COPYING IS PROHIBITED.

waiting for the bathroom as he came out of the shower, coming in the door late at night. He still smelled his father's Old Spice somewhere, his mother's talc.

Sometimes he was so sure one of them was somewhere around him that he thought maybe he was going crazy. His heart hurt him. He wondered if he would ever get better. And though he denied it, he did hate Esther. She was so different from his mother and father. Prejudiced—she admired only those who were white and Presbyterian. Selfish—she wouldn't allow him to use her phone. Complaining—she always had a headache or a backache or a stomachache.

He didn't want to, but he hated her. And he didn't know what to do except lie about it.

Michael hadn't made any friends at his new school, and his teachers barely noticed him. He came home alone every day and usually found Esther on the phone. She kept in close touch with several other women in nearby condominiums. Esther told her friends she didn't understand Michael. She said she knew he must grieve for his parents, but why punish her? She said she thought she might send him away if he couldn't be nicer. She said she didn't deserve this. But when Michael came in the door, she always quickly changed the subject.

One day after school Michael came home with a hermit crab.* He had gone into a pet store, looking for some small, living thing, and hermit crabs were selling for just a few dollars. He'd bought one, and a bowl.

Esther, for a change, was not on the phone when he arrived home. She was having tea and a crescent roll and seemed cheerful. Michael wanted badly to show someone what he had bought. So he showed her.

Esther surprised him. She picked up the shell and poked the long, shiny nail of her little finger at the crab's claws. "Where is he?" she asked.

Michael showed her the crab's eyes peering through the small opening of the shell.

"Well, for heaven's sake, come out of there!" she said to the crab, and she turned the shell upside down and shook it. "Aunt Esther!" Michael grabbed for the shell.

"All right, all right." She turned it right side up. "Well," she said, "what does he do?"

Michael grinned and shrugged his shoulders.

"I don't know," he answered. "Just grows, I guess." His aunt looked at him.

"An attraction to a crab is something I cannot identify with. However, it's fine with me if you keep him, as long as I can be assured he won't grow out of that bowl." She gave him a hard stare.

"He won't," Michael answered. "I promise." ❖

---

* **The hermit crab** is a type of crab that doesn't have a very hard shell. Not a true crab, it uses other animals' old shells for protection. As the hermit crab grows in size, it must find a larger shell.

© GREAT SOURCE. COPYING IS PROHIBITED.

✳ How is Michael similar to another character in a different story in this book? Use your **Response Notes** to make your connection in one sentence.

Michael in "Shells" reminds me of (name of other character) in (name of story) because . . . _____

_____

_____

_____

_____

_____

_____

✳ How does the hermit crab affect the characters in "Shells"?

Michael	Aunt Esther

Making connections
and interacting with the text
help the reader achieve a deeper
understanding of the story.

© GREAT SOURCE. COPYING IS PROHIBITED.

Before reading the rest of the story, think about the hermit crab that Michael brought home. Did you have any idea when he brought it home that it might take on the role of another character in the story? Read about the author to learn why she may have written a role for a hermit crab. In the **Response Notes,** write any connections you notice between the author's life and her writing.

ABOUT THE AUTHOR

It's not surprising that Cynthia Rylant used a hermit crab in her story. She loves animals, and you will find many in her books. Rylant has said that taking walks with her dogs helps her writing. It's always important to see how she uses animals. Some, like Sluggo, become metaphors; others just add interest to the story. Cynthia Rylant has been a teacher, a librarian, and a writer. When she isn't writing, she enjoys watching movies, as well as whales, dolphins, and sea otters. So her attraction to a sea creature is understandable.

You may have read books by Cynthia Rylant, like *Missing May* or *When I Was Young in the Mountains*. She writes for younger children as well as for teenagers and adults. She didn't read much when she was a child. "There just weren't that many books around," she remembers. "No public library, no money to buy books—no book-stores, anyway." Instead, she spent her time playing, something she now says is the best thing for young writers to do. There were some stories available for her in the form of Archie and Jughead comic books and paperback romance novels. So she earned her "training" as a writer with comics from the local drugstore, buying them "three for a quarter—plus Danny Alderman who lived behind me used to trade me a big pile of his for a big pile of mine."

© GREAT SOURCE. COPYING IS PROHIBITED.

✳ **Do you think the hermit crab will help Michael with his problem? In what ways? List your ideas.**

_____

_____

_____

_____

_____

_____

_____

_____

_____

_____

_____

_____

_____

Animal characters, real or imaginary, can add a deeper dimension to a story.

© GREAT SOURCE. COPYING IS PROHIBITED.

An author can let you know what a character is feeling in several different ways. Most times, an author will use more than one of these techniques in a single piece of writing. The author can express a character's feelings by having the character speak directly in dialogue, describing how the character feels, or telling what the character is doing or how he or she is acting. As you read the rest of the story, focus on the how the author conveys Michael's thoughts and feelings.

In the **Response Notes**, jot down clues that show how Michael's feelings are changing.

"Shells" by Cynthia Rylant *(continued)*

Response Notes

The hermit crab moved into the condominium. Michael named him Sluggo and kept the bowl beside his bed. Michael had to watch the bowl for very long periods of time to catch Sluggo with his head poking out of his shell, moving around. Bedtime seemed to be Sluggo's liveliest part of the day, and Michael found it easy to lie and watch the busy crab as sleep slowly came on.

One day Michael arrived home to find Esther sitting on the edge of his bed, looking at the bowl. Esther usually did not intrude in Michael's room, and seeing her there disturbed him. But he stood at the doorway and said nothing.

Esther seemed perfectly comfortable, although she looked over at him with a frown on her face.

"I think he needs a companion," she said.

"What?" Michael's eyebrows went up as his jaw dropped down.

Esther sniffed.

"I think Sluggo needs a girl friend." She stood up. "Where is that pet store?"

Michael took her. In the store was a huge tank full of hermit crabs.

"Oh my!" Esther grabbed the rim of the tank and craned her neck over the side. "Look at them!"

Michael was looking more at his Aunt Esther than at the crabs. He couldn't believe it.

"Oh, look at those shells. You say they grow out of them?" We must stock up with several sizes. See the pink in that one? Michael, look! He's got his little head out!"

Esther was so dramatic—leaning into the tank, her bangle bracelets clanking, earrings swinging, red pumps clicking on the linoleum—that she attracted the attention of everyone in the store. Michael pretended not to know her well.

He and Esther returned to the condominium with a thirty gallon tank and twenty hermit crabs.

© GREAT SOURCE. COPYING IS PROHIBITED.

Michael figured he'd have a heart attack before he got the heavy tank into their living room. He figured he'd die and Aunt Esther would inherit twenty-one crabs and funeral expenses.

But he made it. Esther carried the box of crabs.

"Won't Sluggo be surprised?" she asked happily. "Oh, I do hope we'll be able to tell him apart from the rest. He's their founding father!"

Michael, in a stupor over his Aunt Esther and the phenomenon of twenty-one hermit crabs, wiped out the tank, arranged it with gravel and sticks (as well as the plastic scuba diver Aunt Esther insisted on buying) and assisted her in loading it up, one by one, with the new residents. The crabs were as overwhelmed as Michael. Not one showed its face. Before moving Sluggo from his bowl, Aunt Esther marked his shell with some red fingernail polish so she could distinguish him from the rest. Then she flopped down on the couch beside Michael.

"Oh, what would your mother think, Michael, if she could see this mess we've gotten ourselves into!"

She looked at Michael with a broad smile, but it quickly disappeared. The boy's eyes were full of pain.

"Oh, my," she whispered. "I'm sorry."

Michael turned his head away.

Aunt Esther, who had not embraced anyone in years, gently put her arm about his shoulders.

"I am so sorry, Michael. Oh, you must hate me."

Michael sensed a familiar smell then. His mother's talc. He looked at his aunt.

"No, Aunt Esther." He shook his head solemnly. "I don't hate you."

Esther's mouth trembled and her bangles clanked as she patted his arm. She took a deep, strong breath. "Well, let's look in on our friend Sluggo," she said. They leaned their heads over the tank and found him. The crab, finished with the old home that no longer fit, was coming out of his shell. ❖

✳ **Review your Response Notes. How did Cynthia Rylant convey Michael's feelings to the reader?**

_____

_____

_____

_____

_____

_____

© GREAT SOURCE. COPYING IS PROHIBITED.

✳ In the very last sentence, the author writes: "The crab, finished with the old home that no longer fit, was coming out of his shell." Why would the author end the story this way?

_____

_____

_____

_____

✳ Exchange your idea with a partner. Is your partner's perspective similar to yours or different? In what way?

_____

_____

_____

_____

✳ If the author had continued this story, how would you predict that Michael and his Aunt Esther would get along in the future? Explain why you feel the way you do.

_____

_____

_____

_____

> Authors reveal their characters' thoughts through dialogue, actions, and description.

© GREAT SOURCE. COPYING IS PROHIBITED.

Effective writing starts with a plan. To get started on your own story that includes two characters facing a problem and an animal (or imaginary creature) that could help solve the problem, use this chart to plan your story.

Setting (time and place)

_____

_____

_____

_____

_____

Characters (2)

_____

_____

The problem

_____

_____

_____

_____

Animal or imaginary creature description

_____

_____

_____

How the problem will be solved

_____

_____

_____

_____

© GREAT SOURCE. COPYING IS PROHIBITED.

WRITING THE BEGINNING

✳ Before you write the beginning to your story, exchange the chart you made on page 218 with a writing partner. Respond to each other's ideas and write down at least one good suggestion your partner can use.

_____

_____

_____

_____

_____

_____

_____

_____

✳ Using "Shells" as a model, think of where you will begin your story. Notice how author Rylant began her story in the middle of a situation (Michael had moved in with his aunt).

_____

_____

_____

_____

_____

_____

_____

_____

_____

_____

_____

_____

© GREAT SOURCE. COPYING IS PROHIBITED.

CONTINUING YOUR STORY

Now continue your story, adding an interesting element (a pet like Sluggo or an imaginary creature), who will take the role of a character in the story. Then use specific details to show how the animal helps solve the problem. (For example, in "Shells," a hermit crab must find a new home.) Be sure you have considered the suggestion you received from your writing partner on page 219.

_____

_____

_____

_____

_____

_____

_____

_____

_____

_____

_____

_____

_____

Making a plan for writing is a useful strategy.

© GREAT SOURCE. COPYING IS PROHIBITED.

A very important step in writing is to look at a draft to see how it can be improved. This is called **revision** because you **see** *(vision)* your writing **again** *(re-)*. If possible, set your story aside for a day or two before revising it. You may want to share your story with a writing partner to find more ways to improve it. Use this list before preparing your final copy.

- Does the beginning get my attention so I want to read more? If not, how could I improve it?

- Do I stay on topic? If not, where do I get off topic?

- Do I use vivid verbs to show action? Where are some places that I could use stronger verbs?

- Do I use specific, concrete details and sensory language to make my piece come alive? Where could I use more details?

- Is the ending satisfying? Does it sound "finished"? If not, what could I do to create a better ending?

- Does my dialogue (if I used any) sound realistic? If not, how can I change it?

- Are my sentences complete? Do I use a variety of sentence types and lengths? If not, where do I need to make changes?

- Have I checked my writing for spelling and punctuation errors?

✳ Think about a good title for your story. Why did the author title hers "Shells"? Ask your writing partner if your title captures the meaning of your story.

✳ After you have made changes to your story, make a final, neat copy in your best handwriting or on a computer. Your class may want to publish the stories in a class book, titled *Our Best Short Stories*.

© GREAT SOURCE. COPYING IS PROHIBITED.

A FINAL REFLECTION

In a final reflection, identify one strategy you have perfected during your work with the *Daybook*. Think about whether you have met the most important goal: that you now really *like to* read and write. Write a paragraph reflecting on your growth as a reader and writer.

_____

_____

_____

_____

_____

_____

_____

_____

_____

_____

_____

_____

_____

_____

_____

_____

_____

_____

Reflection is a vital part of learning to read and write effectively.

© GREAT SOURCE. COPYING IS PROHIBITED.

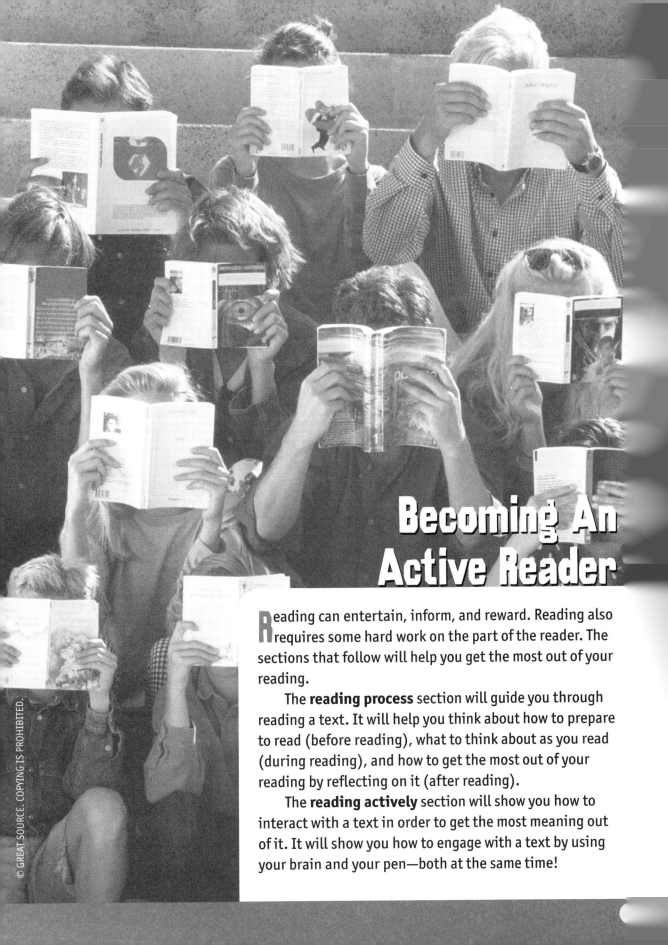

© GREAT SOURCE. COPYING IS PROHIBITED.

Becoming An Active Reader

Reading can entertain, inform, and reward. Reading also requires some hard work on the part of the reader. The sections that follow will help you get the most out of your reading.

The **reading process** section will guide you through reading a text. It will help you think about how to prepare to read (before reading), what to think about as you read (during reading), and how to get the most out of your reading by reflecting on it (after reading).

The **reading actively** section will show you how to interact with a text in order to get the most meaning out of it. It will show you how to engage with a text by using your brain and your pen—both at the same time!

The Reading Process has three parts: **Before Reading, During Reading,** and **After Reading.**

1. BEFORE READING

✳ Preview the Material

Look over the selection before you read. Does the selection look like a short story or other work of fiction? If so, look at the title, introduction, and illustrations. Does the selection look like nonfiction? If so, look for headings, boldfaced words, photos, and captions. Also, ask yourself how the information is organized. Is the author comparing or contrasting information about the topic? Is the information presented in a sequence using signal words like *first, second, third,* and *finally*? Understanding how an author has organized information will help you to recognize key points as you read.

✳ Make Predictions

When you make predictions, you actively connect with the words on the page. Think about what you already know about the subject or the images. Then, think of yourself as a text detective, putting together what you know with new details in the text. Predict what you think will happen: why an event caused something to happen or what might come next in a series of events.

✳ Set a Purpose

Begin by reviewing what you already know about the topic or situation in the text. Then, think about what you want to find out.

QUESTIONS TO ASK YOURSELF BEFORE READING

- Before I read this material, what do I think it is going to be about?
- After looking over the selection, what do I already know about this subject?
- What should I be thinking about as I read?

© GREAT SOURCE. COPYING IS PROHIBITED.

2. DURING READING

※ Engage with the Text

As your eyes look at the words, your brain should be working to make connections between the words and what you already know. Have you had an experience similar to that of one of the characters in a story you are reading? Do you know someone like the character? Have you read another book about the topic? You will also want to connect what you read to the predictions you made before reading. *Confirm, revise, predict again* is a cycle that continues until you finish reading the material. All of these questions will go on inside your head. Sometimes, though, it helps to think out loud or write.

※ Monitor Your Understanding

As you read, stop from time to time and ask yourself, "Do I understand what I just read?" If the text doesn't make sense, there are several steps that you can take.

- Go back and reread the text carefully.
- Read on to see if more information helps you understand.
- Pull together the author's ideas in a summary.
- Retell, or say in your own words, the events that have happened.
- Picture in your mind what the author described.
- Look for context clues or word-structure clues to help you figure out hard words.

This takes some practice. Remember, to be a successful reader, you must be an active reader. Make an effort to check your understanding every so often when you read a new selection.

QUESTIONS TO ASK YOURSELF WHILE YOU ARE READING

- What important details am I finding?
- Which of these ideas seem to be the most important?
- Does this information fit with anything I already know?
- What do I see in my mind as I read this material?
- Do I understand the information in the charts or tables? Does it help me understand what I am reading?

© GREAT SOURCE. COPYING IS PROHIBITED.

3. AFTER READING

✳ Summarize

Reread to locate the most important ideas in the story or essay.

✳ Respond and Reflect

Talk with a partner about what you have read. What did you learn from the text? Were your predictions confirmed? What questions do you still have? Talking about reading helps you better understand what you have read.

✳ Ask Questions

Try asking yourself questions that begin like this:

Can I compare or contrast... evaluate... connect... examine... analyze... relate...

✳ Engage with the Text

Good readers engage with a text all the time, even when they have finished reading. When you tie events in your life or something else you have read to what you are currently reading, you become more involved with your reading. In the process, you are learning more about your values, relationships in your family, and issues in the world around you.

QUESTIONS TO ASK YOURSELF AFTER READING

- What was this article about?
- What was the author trying to tell me?
- Have I learned something that made me change the way I think about this topic?
- Are there parts of this material that I really want to remember?

© GREAT SOURCE. COPYING IS PROHIBITED.

© GREAT SOURCE. COPYING IS PROHIBITED.

Make the effort to stay involved with your reading by reading actively. Your mind should be busy reading the text, making connections, making predictions, and asking questions. Your hand should be busy, too. Keep track of what you are thinking by "reading with your pen." **Write** your reactions to the text or connections that you can make. **Circle** words you don't understand. **Draw** a sketch of a scene. **Underline** or **highlight** an important idea. You may have your own way of reading actively. You may develop a style that works better for you, but here are six common ways of reading actively.

MARK OR HIGHLIGHT The most common way of noting important parts of a text is to write on a sticky note and put it on the page. Or, if you can, mark important parts of a text by highlighting them with a marker, pen, or pencil. You can also use highlighting tape. The highlighted parts should provide a good review of the text.

ASK QUESTIONS Asking questions is a way of engaging the author in conversation. Readers who ask a lot of questions think about the text more and understand it better. "Why is the writer talking about this?" "Is this really true?" "What does that mean?"

REACT AND CONNECT When you read, listen to the author and to yourself. Think about what you are reading and relate it to your own life. Compare and contrast what the text says to what you know.

PREDICT Readers who are involved with the text constantly wonder how things will turn out. They think about what might happen. They check their thoughts against the text and make adjustments. Sometimes the author surprises them! Making predictions helps you stay interested in what you are reading.

VISUALIZE Making pictures in your mind can help you "see" what you are thinking and help you remember. A chart, a sketch, a diagram— any of these can help you "see." Sometimes your picture doesn't match what you think the author is telling you. This is a signal to reread to check your understanding of the text.

CLARIFY As you read, you need to be sure that you understand what is going on in the text. Take time to pull together what you have learned. Try writing notes to clarify your understanding. Another way of checking to see that you understand is to tell someone about what you have read.

GLOSSARY

acrobatic able to move like an acrobat; exceptionally agile

adjacent to next to, connected to

adversity hardship

aftershocks small tremors that often follow an earthquake

aglus hole in a piece of ice where a seal comes up for air when swimming under the ice

alliance partnership

alphabetic having a set of letters, each standing for a sound, that can be used to spell words

anonymous without an identity

apathy a feeling of not caring

Apollo a theater in Harlem

assured promised

at bay cornered

authorities people in charge, such as police officers and firefighters

autobiography an author's story of his or her own life

Ay, Dios Spanish exclamation of surprise or amazement

barbed wire fence wire with many sharp points

barge a large, flat-bottomed boat used to carry heavy loads

barracks a large, plain, temporary building

bear the lash be beaten

belie misrepresent

bellowed yelled

benevolent kind, giving

berserk crazy; out of control

bestowed gave

binary language the basic code of computer programming, which contains only combinations of the numbers 0 and 1

biodegradable capable of breaking down, or decomposing, naturally

bold fearless; brave

bonjour French word for "hello" or "good day"

bountiful plentiful

breadwinner family member who earns most of the money a family needs to survive

brimming full, almost overflowing

brouhaha huge fuss

buffeting pushing as if repeatedly striking

bustled buzzed with activity; was crowded and busy

candidly honestly

carnie mildly insulting slang term for "carnival worker"

cataracts waterfalls

ceramic made from clay

chador [chah DOR] garment worn by women and girls to cover their hair and shoulders

char a type of fish in the trout family

characteristics (of a genre) the features that define a genre

characterization the way an author reveals information about the people, animals, and imaginary creatures in a story

cocoon a protective cover or case, such as that which shelters an animal during its pupa stage

© GREAT SOURCE. COPYING IS PROHIBITED.

commingled mixed

condominium apartment-like house

connection relationship based on similar experiences

consumers those who utilize goods and services

contaminates makes something dirty or impure

context the circumstances or events that make up the environment within which events takes place

conviction a strong belief

convulsion violent upheaval

cooing talking in an overly happy way; similar to "baby talk"

coveted longed for, desired

critical reading and writing strategies skills that involve understanding and evaluating information outside a text one is reading or writing

critics people who write reviews of other people's work

cross-stitch a kind of embroidery

crucial important; essential

crystal high quality glass

cupie-doll an early 1900s doll with a rotund body and a wisp of hair

debilitating weakening

debris remains of something that's been destroyed

defiant defying or showing resistance to authority

details information used to support the main idea of an argument

descriptive language words that capture images

dialogue conversation(s) between characters in a story

discrimination attitudes and actions based on prejudice rather than on an individual's merit

dispel to scatter; drive away

dissever to separate, to cut apart

distinguish tell apart

drawbacks problems or disadvantages

draw conclusions to come up with a summary of a situation based on information given

dully in a depressed or sad way

eddy a small whirlpool; water with a circular motion

eerie spooky, scary

eliminate get rid of

embargo a ban on something

embittered harboring feelings of anger and resentment

emerged came out

emotional language language that evokes feelings

energy-efficient using as little energy as possible

environmentalists people who focus on ways to protect natural resources

epistle poem a letter written as a poem

equilibrium a state of balance

erupted released suddenly

ese Spanish slang for "you." The use here is similar to that in the greeting "Hey, you!"

© GREAT SOURCE. COPYING IS PROHIBITED.

essential important, necessary

exobiologist a biologist who searches for life beyond Earth

extraterrestrial beyond Earth

facts information that can be proved

fantasy a type of fiction featuring imaginary worlds and magical or supernatural events

farm team a minor-league team

fashioning making, forming, shaping

financial security having enough money to live a comfortable life

first-person point of view the telling of a story in which the narrator is one of the characters and calls himself or herself "I"

flank side

floe a large piece of floating ice

foreboding a feeling that something dreadful is about to happen

foreigner a person from another country

fortify strengthen

fortitude strength

fossil fuels energy resources formed in the earth from remains of long-dead plants and animals

founding father the first to start something

fractures breaks

freak show a display of unusual creatures, such as a two-headed dog, commonly found at a fair

French knots on samplers an allusion to a common symbol of home—the words "Home, Sweet Home" cross-stitched in a wall hanging; French knot is a particular type of stitch made with yarn or floss

full throttle to run at top speed

funneled came from various directions toward one point

furrow a long, narrow, shallow trench in the ground

gawked stared in disbelief

generators machines that convert mechanical energy into electrical energy

genre a type of writing

geyser a hot spring that shoots water or steam into the air

girders big beams that support a building or bridge

global view having a broad perspective

gorge deep narrow passage

graphic novel a story presented as a cartoon

grieve mourn

grim serious, gloomy

groping feeling around with fingers or hands

grudge an attitude of anger or bitterness toward someone

half-coy acting shy

historical fiction fiction set in the past, in a time of important historical events

hole in this context, a place where the water swirls very rapidly in a circle, creating suction that is very dangerous for rafters

honeycombs the waxy structures in which bees store honey

horizon line where ground meets sky; in this case, the edges of the area that could be seen

humanity human qualities

© GREAT SOURCE. COPYING IS PROHIBITED.

identity a person's answers to the questions "Who am I?" "Where do I belong?" and "How do I fit in?"

ideogram a picture that represents an idea

impelled moved or urged to do something

impenetrable unable to be passed through

impervious resistant

in a fix in trouble

incinerators a place for burning waste

inevitable impossible to avoid

intensity very strong feeling

interacting with a text to "carry on a conversation" with a text; a strategy for effective reading that involves circling, underlining, and writing notes

interstellar between stars or solar systems

interview a one-on-one meeting in which someone is asked questions about himself or herself

intoxicated excited in an obsessed way

intrude break in on

jangles harsh, metallic sounds

Jesse Semple a character in many of Hughes's stories

Kabul [KAH bul] capital city of Afghanistan

kayak a native American canoe with a wooden frame covered by animal skins and propelled with a paddle

kinsmen relatives, members of one's family

landfall arrival at shore after a journey by water

Langston Hughes a poet (1902–1967) who was an influential presence in the Harlem Renaissance, a movement based in New York City that celebrated African American life and culture

Le bateau est sur l'eau. French for "The boat is on the water."

leach seep into

Lenox and 7th Harlem streets

levitate to rise and float in the air

linoleum a type of floor covering that's like tile

locomotion the ability to move around from place to place

lope run with a steady rhythm

maiden an unmarried woman

make inferences a reading strategy that involves making reasonable guesses by putting together something you have read in a story with something you know from real life; "reading between the lines"

making connections a reading strategy that involves comparing what you are reading to something you already know

Malali [mah LAH lee] legendary young girl who gave Afghani troops the courage to defeat an enemy in 1880

marauding raiding

masonry bricks and stones

meditation deep reflection

menacing threatening

migratory traveling from a colder climate to a warmer one

multiple perspectives different points of view in a story that allow a reader to look at a moment or event from more than one angle

© GREAT SOURCE. COPYING IS PROHIBITED.

muscular dystrophy a fatal disease that gradually weakens all muscles in the body

narrator a storyteller

naysayers people who say something is impossible

obliged to you thank you

obliterated wiped out; obscured

ominously in a threatening way

on the sly secretly

oncologist a doctor who specializes in cancer diagnosis and treatment

oppressiveness heaviness, burden

out of kilter out of order

Oya-oya! Japanese exclamation meaning "my goodness!"

pass a permission form

PCBs chemical compounds that can build up in animal tissue

permeated filled

persistent keeping at it

personal narrative a short prose piece in which a writer expresses personal thoughts and makes connections

perspective the point of view or angle from which you see a subject

persuade to try to convince others to feel the same way you do

persuasive writing writing that attempts to persuade a reader of the validity of an argument by using persuasive details

pertinacity ability to stick with it

phenomenon unusual occurrence

pictograph a picture that represents a familiar object

pivoting turning around

point of view the vantage point from which a story is told

plot how the characters and events in a story are connected

prediction an educated guess about upcoming events that is based on background knowledge and clues from the present

prejudiced feeling strongly about something, regardless of any facts to the contrary

Presbyterian member of a particular Protestant church

pretense pretending something isn't what it is

purpose an author's intent in writing a piece

queasy having nausea

queue a ponytail once worn by Chinese men

quiver tremble or shake

ramshackle rundown, not sturdy

raza-style part-Spanish for a hand-shake style expressive of a Latino culture

reading for meaning reading with focus and effort to discover and understand an author's message

rebellious tending to go against the rules

recounted reviewed; retold

reflecting taking time to think about what you have read

relish a feeling of enthusiasm or delight

Renaissance man a person who is accomplished in many areas, both arts and sciences.

© GREAT SOURCE. COPYING IS PROHIBITED.

repertoire a performer's collection of abilities

respite a short time of rest

revision looking at a draft again in order to find ways to improve it

riddled filled with holes; perforated

rouge makeup that reddens cheeks

runt a scrawny creature. The runt of a litter of puppies is the smallest.

saludo de vato Spanish for a special head nod expressive of a Latino culture

scavengers animals that eat dead and decaying plants and animals

scholars people who make a living doing research in colleges and universities

Scotland Yard/MI 5 security forces of the British government

second-person point of view the telling of a story in which the reader is one of the characters and is the "you" referred to in the story

seminal influential; important development

sensory language language that appeals to the reader's senses

sepulcher a grave or tomb

seraphs angels, heavenly beings

setting the time and place of a story

shalwar kameez [SHAHL wahr kah MEEZ] a long, loose shirt and trousers worn by either a man or a woman

sheepish embarrassed

shrine a place for worship

simile a technique of figurative language in which the characteristics of one thing are described in terms of something else using the word like or as

solemnly seriously

somber darkening

speared in this context, to position precisely

spooked scared away; startled

sprint burst of speed

staggering overwhelming, unbelievable

steadfast firm, constant, unwavering

steeples pointed towers on churches

stereotypic not original or having no individuality; trite

stitching a decoration made from thread

story elements the essential parts that make up a story

strategic reading using a repertoire of skills and strategies to make decisions about how to approach texts

strivings intense efforts

structural mitigation techniques ways of making buildings safer

summarize to find the main idea of a text and restate it in your own words

Sweet Flypaper of Life a book of Harlem photographs by Hughes and photographer Ray DeCarava

symbolism the use of symbols to communicate ideas

symbols images or objects that represent other things

syllabic having a set of symbols, each standing for a sound

talc powder

© GREAT SOURCE. COPYING IS PROHIBITED.

Taliban (TAL ih bahn) ruling party in Afghanistan from 1996–2001. A member of the party is a Talib (TAL eeb).

tangible something that can be touched

tarp a piece of heavy canvas

taunts insulting remarks intended to anger

tempest storm

tenement a rundown building where poor people live

theme the main topic or message that is explored through the characters and plot of a story

thermal a column of warm, rising air. Thermals form over hot, flat surfaces, such as the floor of a canyon, offering soaring birds and hang gliders a literal lift.

thermostats devices that control temperature

thicket a place where plants grow very close together

third-person point of view the telling of a story in which the narrator is not part of the story: a limited third-person narrator reveals the thoughts and feelings of only one character; an omniscient third-person narrator reveals the thoughts and feelings of several characters

thrashing a beating

tiered stacked up

toddle to walk unsteadily like a toddler

toshak (TOH shawk) a mattress used as a bed, chair, or couch; similar to a futon

toxic poisonous

trauma emotional shock

tremendous great

Trés bien. Parlez-vous français? French for "Very good. Do you speak French?"

tundra a treeless area between the icecap and the tree line of Arctic regions

turbulence boisterous or unsettled air

Underground formal name for London's subway system

undulate roll like a wave

unwonted unusual

variometer an instrument used to monitor altitude during flight

ventured forth set out on a new adventure

ventured tried, said

visual information messages presented with visual images

visualizing a reading strategy in which a reader makes pictures in his or her mind of a text

visual text a collection of visual images that present a coherent message

whiff an inhaling of air; in this context "take a whiff" means to smell something

winced to have shrunk or drawn back, as if in pain

wound a cut or tear in the outer layer of a plant

wretched badly made

© GREAT SOURCE. COPYING IS PROHIBITED.

© GREAT SOURCE. COPYING IS PROHIBITED.

10 Excerpt from "The Computer Date" from *A Summer Life* by Gary Soto. Copyright © 1990 by University Press of New England.

11, 13, 16 "Seventh Grade" from *Baseball in April and Other Stories,* copyright © 1990 by Gary Soto, reprinted by permission of Harcourt, Inc.

19 "Oranges" from *New And Selected Poems* © 1995 by Gary Soto. Used with permission of Chronicle Books, LLC, San Francisco. Visit ChronicleBooks.com.

22 Excerpt from *Living Up the Street* by Gary Soto (Dell, 1991), © 1985 by Gary Soto. Used by permission of the author.

26, 29 From *The Breadwinner* by Deborah Ellis. Copyright © 2001. Used by permission of Groundwood Books.

35 "Vietnam War Memorial" from "Journey Through Hartsong" by Mattie J.T. Stepanek. Used by permission of Hyperion Books.

40, 42, 44 Excerpts from *Year of Impossible Goodbyes* by Sook Nyul Choi. Copyright © 1991 by Sook Nyul Choi. Reprinted by permission of Houghton Mifflin Company. All rights reserved.

45, 48 "Thank You, Ma'am" from *Short Stories* by Langston Hughes. Copyright © 1996 by Ramona Bass and Arnold Rampersad. Used by permission of Hill and Wang, a division of Farrar, Straus and Giroux, LLC.

54 With permission of Robert W. Peterson and *Boys' Life,* April 1997, published by the Boy Scouts of America.

58 Used by permission of Primedia History Group.

62 Copyright © 1996 by Sharon Robinson. Reprinted by permission of HarperCollins Publishers.

65 Lucille Clifton, "jackie robinson" from *Good Woman: Poems and a Memoir 1969-1980.* Copyright © 1987 by Lucille Clifton. Reprinted with the permission of BOA Editions, Ltd., www.BOAEditions.org.

70, 73, 75 "Poem Book", "Name all the People", "Line Break Poem", "Epistle Poem", from *Locomotion* by Jacqueline Woodson, copyright © 2003 by Jacqueline Woodson. Used by permission of G.P. Putnam's Sons, A Division of Penguin Young Readers Group, A Member of Penguin Group (USA) Inc., 345 Hudson Street, New York, NY 10014. All rights reserved.

77 "Mother to Son" from *Collected Poems* by Langston Hughes. Used by permission of Random House Inc.

80 "Long Live Langston" by Wesley Boone from *Bronx Masquerade* by Nikki Grimes. Used by permission of Penguin Putnam.

82 From *Bronx Masquerade* by Nikki Grimes. Used by permission of Penguin Putnam.

86 "The Princess of Light" from *The Dancing Kettle and Other Japanese Folktales* retold by Yoshiko Uchida, illustrated by Richard C. Jones.

90 From *The Invisible Thread* by Yoshiko Uchida. Reprinted with the permission of Simon & Schuster Books for Young Readers, an imprint of Simon & Schuster Children's Publishing Division. Copyright © 1991 Yoshiko Uchida.

93 From *Journey Home* by Yoshiko Uchida. Reprinted with the permission of Margaret K. McElderry Books, an imprint of Simon & Schuster Children's Publishing Division. Text copyright © 1978 Yoshiko Uchida.

96 From *Desert Exile: The Uprooting of a Japanese-American Family* by Yoshiko Uchida. First published by University of Washington Press, 1982. Reprinted with permission.

99 From a conversation with Yoshiko Uchida. Reprinted with permission.

102 "Birthday Box," copyright © 1995 by Jane Yolen. First appreared in *Birthday Surprises: Ten Great Stories to Unwrap,* published by Morrow Junior Books. Reprinted by permission of Curtis Brown, Ltd.

107 "The Key to Everything" from *The Complete Love Poems of May Swenson.* Copyright © 1991, 2003 by The Literary Estate of May Swenson. Reprinted by the permission of Houghton Mifflin Company. All rights reserved.

109 www.JaneYolen.com, copyright © 2000 by Jane Yolen. Reprinted by permission of Curtis Brown, Ltd.

113 Excerpt from *Island of the Blue Dolphins* by Scott O'Dell. Copyright © 1960, renewed 1988 by Scott O'Dell. Reprinted by permission of Houghton Mifflin Company. All rights reserved.

118 Excerpts from *Ice Drift,* copyright © 2005 by Theodore Taylor, reprinted by permission of Harcourt, Inc.

121 Reprinted with the permission of Atheneum Books for Young Readers, an imprint of Simon & Schuster Children's Publishing Division, from *True Believer* by Virginia Euwer Wolff. Copyright © 2001 Virginia Euwer Wolff.

124 From *The Terrorist* by Caroline B. Cooney. Published by Scholastic Press/Scholastic Inc. Copyright © 1997 by Caroline B. Cooney. Reprinted by permission.

129 "Homeless," copyright © 1987 by Anna Quindlen, from *Living Out Loud* by Anna Quindlen. Used by permission of Random House, Inc.

134, 137 Courtesy of Cartoon Books.

140 NBM Publishing.

148, 151 Text copyright © 1995 by Eagle Productions. Used by permission of HarperCollins Publishers.

151 From "Three Fearful Days", edited by Malcolm Barker. Used be permission of Sunset Publishing Corp.

154 Copyright © 1975 by Lawrence Yep. Used by permission of HarperCollins Publishers.

160 © Copyright The American National Red Cross. All rights reserved.

164 Roach, John & Ives, Sara/National Geographic

167, 175 Excerpt from *You Are the Earth*. Copyright © 1990 by David Suzuki and Kathy Vanderlinden. Published by Breystone Books, a division of Douglas & McIntyre Ltd. Reprinted by permission of the publisher.

169 Excerpt from *Odyssey*'s April 2004 issue: Future Power, © 2004, Carus Publishing Company, published by Cobblestone Publishing, 30 Grove Street, Suite C, Peterborough, NH 03458. All Rights Reserved. Used by permission of the author.

172 From *Harvest for Hope* by Jane Goodall with Gary McAvoy and Gail Hudson. Copyright © 2005 by Jane Goodall and Gary McAvoy. By permission of Warner Books, Inc.

179 "The Last Page" from *A History of Reading* by Alberto Manguel, copyright © 1996 by Alberto Manguel. Used by permission fo Penguin, a division of Penguin Group (USA) Inc.

179 Reprinted by Consent of Brooks Permissions.

182, 184 Reprinted by permission of Don Lago.

190 "The Road Not Taken" from *The Poetry of Robert Frost* edited by Edward Connery Lathem. Copyright © 1969 by Henry Holt and Company. Reprinted by permission of Henry Holt and Company, LLC.

194, 197, 200 Text Copyright © 1998 by Will Hobbs. Used by permission of HarperCollins Publishers.

202 Reprinted with the permission of Atheneum Books for Young Readers, an imprint of Simon & Schuster Children's Publishing Division from *Kokopelli's Flute* by Will Hobbs. Copyright © 1995 Will Hobbs.

204 Reprinted with the permission of Atheneuem Books for Young Readers, an imprint of Simon & Schuster Children's Publishing Division from *Downriver* by Will Hobbs. Copyright © 1991 Will Hobbs.

207 Reprinted with the permission of Atheneuem Books for Young Readers, an imprint of Simon & Schuster Children's Publishing Division from *Bearstone* by Will Hobbs. Copyright © 1989 Will Hobbs.

210, 215 "Shells" from *Every Living Thing* by Cynthia Rylant. Reprinted with the permission of Simon & Schuster Books for Young Readers, an imprint of Simon & Schuster Children's Publishing Division. Copyright © 1985 Cynthia Rylant

ILLUSTRATIONS

137: © Great Source; **142 *m*:** © Laszlo Kubinyi. Reprinted by permission of Houghton Mifflin Company. All rights reserved.
All additional art created by AARTPACK, Inc.

PHOTOGRAPHY

Photo Research AARTPACK, Inc.

Unit 1 **9:** © Duncan Smith/Getty Images; **10*t*:** © Donna Day/Getty Images; **10*b*:** © Itstock/InMagine; **11:** © Donna Day/Getty; **12:** © Royalty-Free/Corbis; **13:** © Royalty-Free/Corbis; **14:** © Tom Merton/Getty; **15:** © Tom Merton/Getty; **16:** © Getty Images; **17:** © Photodisc/InMagine; **18:** © Getty Images; **19:** © Photodisc/InMagine; **20:** © Photodisc/InMagine; **21:** © Royalty-Free/Corbis; **22:** © Royalty-Free/Corbis; **23:** © Royalty-Free/Corbis

Unit 2 **25:** © Julio Lopez Saguar/Getty; **26:** © Paula Bronstein/Getty; **27:** © Thorne Anderson/Corbis; **28*l*:** © Paula Bronstein/Getty; **28*r*:** © Paula Bronstein/Getty; **29:** © Le Segretain Pascal/Corbis Sygma; **30:** © Le Segretain Pascal/Corbis Sygma; 31: © Paula Bronstein/Getty; **32:** © Hulton Archive/Getty; **33:** © Bettmann/Corbis; **34:** © Royalty-Free/Corbis; **35*t*:** © Royalty-Free/Corbis; **35*b*:** © Joyce Naltchayan/Getty; **36:** © Royalty-Free/Corbis; **37:** © 1993 PhotoDisc, Inc.; **38:** © 1993 PhotoDisc, Inc.

Unit 3 **39:** © Debra McClinton/Getty; **40:** © Getty Images; **41:** © Getty Images; **42:** © Royalty-Free/Corbis; **43:** © Megumi Takamura/Getty; **44:** © Photodisc/InMagine; **45:** © Stockbyte/InMagine; **46:** © Getty Images; **47:** © Getty Images; **48:** © Jules Frazier/Getty; **49:** © Comstock, Inc. 1998; **50:** © Jules Frazier/Getty; **51:** © Tom Morrison/Getty; **52:** © Royalty-Free/Corbis

Unit 4 **53:** © Bettmann/Corbis; **54:** © Royalty-Free/Corbis; **55:** © Bettmann/Corbis; **56:** © Comstock/InMagine; **58:** © Royalty-Free/Corbis; **59:** © Bettmann/ Corbis; **60:** © Royalty-Free/Corbis; **61:** © Royalty-Free/Corbis; **62:** © Michael Matisse/Getty; **63:** © Phil Schermeister/Corbis; **64:** © Michael Matisse/Getty; **65t:** © Kaz Chiba/1997 PhotoDisc, Inc.; **65b:** © Bettmann/Corbis; **66:** © Royalty-Free/Corbis; **67:** © Bettmann/Corbis; **68:** © Flip Schulke/Corbis

Unit 5 **69:** © Royalty-Free/Corbis; **70:** © Royalty-Free/Corbis; **71:** © Royalty-Free/Corbis; **72:** © Alexander Walter/Getty; **73:** © Alexander Walter/Getty; **74:** © Ultraviolent/Getty; **75t:** © Royalty-Free/Corbis; **75b:** © Royalty-Free/Corbis; **76:** © Royalty-Free/Corbis; **77:** © Getty Images; **78:** © Getty Images; **79:** © Getty Images; **80:** © Getty Images; **81t:** © Sami Sarkis/Getty; **81b:** © Sami Sarkis/Getty; **82t:** © Royalty-Free/Corbis; **82b:** © Royalty-Free/Corbis; **83:** © Royalty-Free/Corbis; **84:** © Royalty-Free/Corbis

Unit 6 **85:** © Corbis; **86:** © Andrew Garn/Getty; **87:** © Jeremy Maude/Getty; **88:** © Jeremy Maude/Getty; **89:** © Getty Images; **90:** © Corbis (U.S. War Relocation Authority); **91:** © Santokh Kochar/Getty; **92:** © Bettmann/Corbis; **93:** © Corbis; **94l:** © Seattle Post-Intelligencer Collection; Museum of History and Industry/Corbis; **94r:** © Seattle Post-Intelligencer Collection; Museum of History and Industry/Corbis; **95:** © Getty Images; **96t:** © Brandxpictures/InMagine; **96b:** © Special Collections Dept., J. Willard Marriott Lbrary, University of Utah; **98:** © Brand X pictures/InMagine; **99:** © Jeremy Maude/Getty

Unit 7 **100:** © Jeremy Maude/Getty; **101:** © Hulton Archive/Getty; **102:** © Getty Images; **103:** © Getty Images; **104:** © Stockdisc/InMagine; **105:** © Getty Images; **106:** © Jan Stromme/Getty; **107:** © Royalty-Free/Corbis; **108:** © Jan Stromme/Getty;

109: © Royalty-Free/Corbis; **110:** © Royalty-Free/Corbis; **111:** © 1993 PhotoDisc, Inc.; **112:** © Tom Brakefield/Getty; **113:** © Royalty-Free/Corbis; **114:** © Tom Brakefield/Getty; **115:** © Royalty-Free/Corbis; **116:** © Image Source/Getty

Unit 8 **117:** © Brian Bailey/Getty; **118:** © Image100/InMagine; **119:** © Image100/InMagine; **120:** © Getty Images; **121:** © Janis Christie/Getty; **122:** © Janis Christie/Getty; **123t:** © MedioImages/Getty; **123r:** © MedioImages/Getty; **124:** © Terry Vine/Getty; **125:** © Digital Vision/Getty; **126:** © Ryan McVay/Getty; **127:** © Alexander Benz/zefa/Corbis; **128:** © Digital Vision/Getty; **129:** © Terry Vine/Getty; **130l:** © Terry Vine/Getty; **130r:** © Terry Vine/Getty; **131:** © Kevin Forest/Getty; **132:** © Kevin Forest/Getty

Unit 9 **133:** © Photonica/Getty; **134t:** © Image Source/Getty; **134b:** © Image Source/Getty; **136:** © Image Source/Getty; **137t:** © Photodisc Green/Getty; **138b:** © 2005 Comstock Images; **139:** © Image Source/Getty; **140l:** © Spencer Grant/PhotoEdit; **143:** © Comstock Images; **143t:** © MedioImages/Getty; **143m:** © MedioImages/Getty; **143b:** © 1993 PhotoDisc, Inc.; **144:** © Digital Vision/Getty; **145:** © Digital Vision/Getty; **146:** © Digital Vision/Getty

Unit 10 **147:** © Bettmann/Corbis; **148:** © InterNetwork Media/Getty; **149:** © 1999 PhotoDisc, Inc.; **150:** © InterNetwork Media/Getty; **151:** © Getty Images; **152:** © Bettmann/Corbis; **154:** © Royalty-Free/Corbis; **155:** © Royalty-Free/Corbis; **156:** © Royalty-Free/Corbis; **157:** © 1999 PhotoDisc, Inc.; **158l:** © 1999 PhotoDisc, Inc.; **158m:** © Bettmann/Corbis; **159t:** © Getty Images; **159r:** © 1999 PhotoDisc, Inc.; **160t:** © Spencer Grant/PhotoEdit; **160b:** © 1999 PhotoDisc, Inc.; **161:** © Getty Images; **162:** © Brand X Pictures

Unit 11 **163:** © Photodisc/InMagine; **164:** © Royalty-Free/Corbis; **165:** © Royalty-Free/Corbis; **166:** © Tracy Montana/PhotoLink/Getty; **167:** © Tracy Montana/PhotoLink/Getty; **168:** © Pete Starman/Getty; **169:** © Tom Brakefield/Getty; **170:** © 1993 photodisc, Inc.; **171:** © Brand X Pictures/InMagine; **172:** © 1993 photodisc, Inc.; **173:** © Philip Wallick/Corbis; **174:** © Royalty-Free/Corbis; **175t:** © Russell Illig/Getty; **175b:** © Royalty-Free/Corbis; **176:** © Getty Images

© GREAT SOURCE. COPYING IS PROHIBITED.

Unit 12 177: © Royalty-Free/Corbis; **178:** © Getty Images; **179:** © Flip Schulke/Corbis; **180:** © Getty Images; **181:** © Royalty-Free/Corbis; **182t:** © Nick Koudis/Getty; **182b:** © Nick Koudis/Getty; **183:** © R H Productions/Getty; **184:** © Photodisc/InMagine; **185:** © Chad Baker/Ryan McVay/Getty; **186:** © Brandxpictures/InMagine; **187:** © Tony Sweet/Getty; **188:** © Ingram/InMagine; **189:** © Tony Sweet/Getty; **190t:** © Royalty-Free/Corbis; **190b:** © Royalty-Free/Corbis; **191:** © Royalty-Free/Corbis; **192:** © William Manning/Corbis

Unit 13 193: © Brandxpictures/InMagine; **194:** © Jack Hollingsworth/Getty; **195:** © Pixtal/InMagine; **196:** © Royalty-Free/Corbis; **197:** © Royalty-Free/Corbis; **199:** © Royalty-Free/Corbis; **200:** © Ablestock/InMagine; **201:** © Ablestock/InMagine; **204:** © Photodisc/InMagine;

205: © Getty Images; **206:** © Ken Redding/Corbis; **207:** © Royalty-Free/Corbis; **208:** © Royalty-Free/Corbis

Unit 14 209: © Royalty-Free/Corbis; **210:** © Kaz chiba/Getty Images; **211:** © Creatas Images/2006 Jupiterimages Corporation; **212:** © 2004 Comstock ImagesLLC; **213b:** © Creatas Images/2006 Jupiterimages Corporation; **213r:** © Royalty-Free/Corbis; **214:** © Kaz chiba/Getty Images; **215:** © Ken Usami/Getty; **216:** © 2004 Comstock ImagesLLC; **217:** © 2001 Brand X Pictures; **218:** © Kaz chiba/Getty Images; **219:** © Kaz chiba/Getty Images; **220:** © Ken Usami/Getty; **221:** © TRBfoto/Getty; **222:** © 2001 Brand X Pictures

Becoming an Active Reader 223: © Photodisc Green/Getty; **224–226:** © Kaz chiba/Getty Images; **227:** © Lonely Planet Images/Getty

© GREAT SOURCE. COPYING IS PROHIBITED.

© GREAT SOURCE. COPYING IS PROHIBITED.

© GREAT SOURCE. COPYING IS PROHIBITED.